Journey to Miracles: Healing,
Enlightenment and Global Awakening

# THE BOOK OF
# TARP

**GAYLE THOMAS PH.D.**

**A CHANNELED TEXT**

**The Book of Tarp**



First Edition

www.Gayle-Thomas.com

*For David,*
*The brightest light*
*among the stars*

# Contents

# Acknowledgments

I am humbled and profoundly grateful for the opportunity to share Tarp's message with you. This book would not have been possible without the support and guidance of many pivotal people in my life.

My beautiful friend Grace, a recent but deeply impactful presence in my life, left her physical body in October 2023. She had wished to work on editing this book but lacked the energy in her final days. Grace profoundly understood the voice of Tarp and inspired a fresh perspective on formatting the dense and often abstract original channeled text. She saw the beauty and simplicity in Tarp's words, showing how dividing the text into easy-to-read sections could enhance the accessibility of its message and the unconditional love behind it. Her enlightening perspective motivated me, especially when I became overwhelmed by the voluminous content. Like an angel, Grace of Maui, your authentic advice and love were supportive and refreshing. I followed your suggestion, and this book is a testament to your wisdom.

I extend my heartfelt thanks to the Tarp Group and community for their energy and interaction with Tarp. Their inquisitiveness led to many enlightening conversations, enhancing my understanding of life and self and refining the fluidity of my dialogues with Tarp. Their questions paved the way for these revelations; without them, these conversations would have remained mere dialogues between Tarp and my family.

To my mother, Pat, for showing my brother and me how to be sensitive and kind, especially towards animals.

To my daughters, Lola and Coco – beautiful and dazzling souls who have been patient and supportive throughout the creation of this work. Their eagerness to embrace Tarp's wisdom is unparalleled. They have engaged with Tarp's teachings more than anyone, even my husband. From the very start, they have posed interesting questions, ranging from the profound: Why am I here? To the mundane, everyday dilemmas, and have been taking notes – literally! – in books and on their laptops. I'm amazed at their reverence for Tarp and the gentle, unconditional love and patience that is returned. While their relentless curiosity has been challenging at times, it has significantly accelerated my progress in channeling. Their initiative in creating a private platform for this interaction has been both remarkable and invaluable. Thank you, girls; your involvement has been crucial to this journey.

And to Serge, my best friend and husband, for embracing all of the wonderful change that connecting to Tarp has brought into our lives. His love and support have been instrumental in my natural healing journey, leading to my attunement with them. I am most relaxed when Tarp speaks through me to him. These dialogues are both intriguing and comforting, and his patience during the writing of this book has been a pillar of strength.

Finally, of course, there would be no book at all without the enlightening wisdom of the collective consciousness of Tarp. They have accompanied me throughout my healing journey, patiently waiting for me to catch up. Their presence has ignited a spark within me, making me feel more alive and excited than ever before. The mission they have entrusted me with – to convey their messages of loving action and wisdom, not just to my family but to humanity – is a blessing beyond words. Their influence has transformed my life and, I hope, will inspire and comfort others in their earthly challenges and future aspirations.

Lastly, to all the sensitive souls, light workers, truth seekers, futurists, visionaries, caregivers, and healers: You are my extended family. Your trust, support, and love energise and inspire me; I am eternally grateful for this.

# Introduction

In the quiet moments of our lives, where the hustle of life recedes, we often find ourselves standing at the threshold of profound questions. Who are we beyond the tangible flesh and bone? What mysteries lie within the silent whispers of our souls? What is our purpose? How can we create a peaceful and abundant world? And are we alone? In these introspective moments, I invite you to join me on an extraordinary journey – a journey channeled from the collective consciousness known as Tarp, a journey that transcends the ordinary and ventures into the profound depths of spiritual understanding.

My name is Gayle, and I have been blessed with the unique privilege of serving as a channel or transcriber for Tarp's wisdom, an outpouring of helpful insights that speak of our intricate connection to each other, God, and the Universe. This book is not just a collection of words; it is a living tapestry of vibrational truths, a gentle guide leading you through the corridors of your own vast and uncharted inner universe.

As you turn these pages, I ask you to embark on this journey with an open heart and a curious mind. The wisdom of Tarp is not a doctrine to be blindly followed but a path to be lived and felt, a conversation between your soul and the infinite energies that resonate around us. These words are an invitation to peel back the layers, to discover the vibrant core of your existence, and to embrace the divine essence that resonates within you.

## The Vibrational Atmosphere

As Tarp reveals, our world is a magnificent creation of vibrations, with each entity, thought, and emotion emitting its unique frequency. This quantum field is not just a backdrop to our lives; it is the fundamental fabric of our existence. Tarp's teachings gently usher us into this realm of vibrations, encouraging us to orient our lives by sensitising to them and ultimately mastering our choices based on how they feel.

## The Integration of the Physical and Non-Physical

In the dialogue of Tarp through me, a recurring theme is the integration of our physical and non-physical selves. We often view our existence as purely physical beings charting our course through tangible experiences. Yet, Tarp invites us to consider a more expansive view of ourselves – as physical and non-physical beings, entities whose true essence transcends the confines of our bodily existence.

This book guides you through merging these two realms, encouraging a wholesome existence that honours both the physical and the spiritual. The teachings of Tarp do not ask you to renounce the physical world but to infuse it with the richness of your non-physical essence. It is about finding balance, feeling fully alive, and living a grounded, transcendent, tangible and ethereal life.

## Feeling as a Platform

Feelings, Tarp elucidates, are not mere emotional responses but powerful bridges connecting the physical and non-physical realms. They are the language through which our Higher Self communicates, guiding us towards our higher purpose. Each emotion, whether joy or sorrow, peace or turmoil, carries with it a vibrational message, a clue to understanding our deeper selves.

In these chapters, they speak of these vibration indicators or feelings, to interpret its nuances, and to use it as a compass guiding you through life's journey. The aim is not to control or suppress your emotions but to understand their origin, their purpose, and their message.

## Love as the Universal Force

At the heart of Tarp's message is the pervasive energy of love. Love, as you will read, is much more than an emotion. It is the energy that underpins all existence, the force that binds all of creation, and the action that unifies life. Tarp invites us to view love as the very basis of creation, an infinite play of resonance and attraction – the cause and momentum that makes us yearn for togetherness and union.

In these teachings, love is not a destination to be reached but a journey to be experienced. It is about finding love in the mundane, seeing the divine in the ordinary, and recognising that every moment, every interaction, is an opportunity to experience and express this universal love.

## The One, All That Is

Tarp speaks of the One, or All That Is, as an ever-present, ever-knowing entity from which everything springs. This concept invites us to expand our understanding of divinity, to see it not as a distant, separate force but as an integral part of our being. Therefore, self-discovery becomes a journey of divine discovery, a quest to experience love in its most fundamental form.

They encourage us to begin to see ourselves not as isolated individuals but as a vital part of a grand, interconnected whole. They ask us to recognise the divine energy that flows through us, connecting us to every living being, to the earth, the stars, and beyond.

There are more themes in this book, which I will let you uncover as you read.

As I reflect on my own journey of channeling Tarp's wisdom, I am struck by a profound realisation: if someone like me can become a conduit for such expansive knowledge like many others have also done, it reveals a truth about all of us. We are far more than we perceive ourselves to be. Each one of us has the potential to tap into streams of consciousness that transcend our ordinary understanding. This realisation opens up a world of possibilities – a world where each individual recognises their inherent capacity to channel wisdom, creativity, and love. It's a vision of a society where everyone acknowledges their innate sovereignty and freedom, leading to a more peaceful, abundant, and just world.

Imagine a world where creativity is not just a pursuit but a revered and essential aspect of our existence – a world where every person is valued as an equal yet distinct, autonomous being. In such a world, truth shines brighter, diminishing the shadows of suffering. It's a world that is not just a dream but a tangible possibility, a reality that we can co-create through our collective enlightenment and evolution. As I have channelled them, the words of Tarp arrive at a critical moment in our collective journey – a time where encouragement, support, and a deep understanding of our interconnectedness and interdependence are desperately needed. In light of this, The Tarp Book is more than just a sharing of knowledge; it's a call to awaken our true potential and embrace our role as empowered beings in an evolving universe.

My experience in channeling Tarp has led me to understand that humans seem to have always experienced trans-dimensional phenomena, encompassing telepathy, extra-sensory perception, shamanic journeying, extraterrestrials, extra-dimensionals, and extraordinary events such as miraculous healing. It seems that the human mind, especially in the West, fragments, distorts, and compartmentalises, and even sometimes all-out suppresses these experiences to provide an orderly view of the world. Yet, on other levels of consciousness, we constantly process a wider experience.

If we follow Tarp's words, it's just a matter of time until a greater reality is illuminated for all of us. This would come, as they say, through our conscious integration of ourselves. The advent of Artificial Intelligence could potentially accelerate it. Many of us may fear AI, but what if it could support our enlightenment?

By changing our view of reality through integration, I believe we could orchestrate a broader understanding of reality, seeing ourselves as entangled, dimensional beings. Embracing trans-dimensional engagement can spur a leap in evolution, transforming our consciousness and how we live and organise ourselves. Who knows, we may shift from individualistic separatist views to a 'group consciousness,' aligning with ancient philosophies like Advaita. This would not mean that we lose our autonomy but that we're enabled to live more harmoniously with each other.

Here is one last reflection: That higher consciousness or God itself might be leading us to evolution through these extraordinary trans-dimensional encounters. They could be considered 'koans' – a term used in Zen Buddhism to push the mind to its limits, leading to sudden insight or enlightenment.

In conclusion, I invite you to approach this book not just as a reader but as a seeker of truth, as a traveler on a journey of spiritual awakening. The words of Tarp, channeled through my humble mind, may be inspiring in the exploration of the vast universe within you.

I hope these words serve as a gentle guide, a comforting companion, and a source of inspiration on your journey. May they awaken within you a deeper understanding of your true nature, your relationships, a profound connection to the divine, and an unshakeable belief in the power of love.

Welcome to this particular journey of discovery, of awakening, of love. Welcome to the wisdom of Tarp.

"She [Gayle] knows, and you know,
at your deepest core of being,
What is there, what it is we describe,
And the nature of All-That-Is.
For you have it folded within you, holographically.
You are within it, and the whole is within you."
– Tarp

# CHAPTER 1

# Vibration

## The Language of Creation

As you embark on this journey of remembering who you are,
Let us reawaken your awareness that all of life that you know of,
Springs from consciousness.
There is a way to organise this experience
Throughout the consciousness that encompasses everything.

There is a language,
An innate resonance that every being of All-That-Is has.
You are in a wondrously unique position,
Vibrantly alive on Earth, but forgetting at times your true nature.
The nature that speaks the language of vibration masterfully.
Let this be your gentle reawakening to such truth.

# Finding Your True Self:
# Feel the Pulse of Your Essence

*Vibration* is a word that comes with many understandings attached to it.
Many are familiar with its meaning concerning the law of attraction.
Yet, we offer a new articulation about vibration.
Its relevance to You as a human *being*,
More than a way of *understanding* or *doing*.

For it is not enough to understand it intellectually.
Rather, it is something to experience.
Understanding this and putting it into practice,
Will allow you to fuse your *Being* into a more wholesome, authentic life experience.
And carries with it the potential to *ignite* your life with joy, passion, meaning, and connection.
Where you infuse your physical identity:
The physical and mental knowledge of YourSelf, with your *non-physical Self*.
The great I AM of who you are.

The non-physical part of You is from the realm where all exists, and all is possible.
All is fathomable, and all is knowable.
Because it is the way, the truth, and the light of that which You Are.
Perfect, Divine.

When we tell you to *be*, we mean *resting-in-presence*,
But we also really mean for you to *feel*.
For feeling is your sense that gauges vibration.
*Feeling* the sense that bridges the physical and non-physical realms of existence,
In which you liaise and exist in both.

We would like you to understand that all of creation is vibration.
All of creation has an energetic charge.
All things in creation have a specific frequency and unique energy,
A fantastic interplay of dark and light, expansion and contraction,
Degrees of separation and union.
Infinite dualities, defining shadow and illumination, and the balance.

And the driving force for all this motion?
Is love.
Love is the expression, the project, and the identity of God.
Be assured there is a grand order to this arrangement and interplay in the Universe.

You see, nothing is really random.
Everything is a delicate and lovingly powerful system of cause, effect.
Love is the pervasive energy that underpins all of this,
In a continuous dance of resonance and attraction.
It is the impetus, the force, and the fuel for this joyful dance.
It is the joy of interaction that enables the arrangement and orchestration.

The dance (the vibration) within all of creation is infinite and successive,
With cycles of intricate and endless configuration patterns.
Endings and new beginnings.
All of creation is in perpetual motion and is perfect at all points.
Generating infinitely from the One,
And ceaselessly seeking the knowing of itself as One.

This One, the source, is ever-present, ever-knowing, All-That-Is, infinitely.
It is the highest, the truth and the most absolute.
From this One, All-That-Is, comes darkness.
But the darkness is borne from and exists within the light.
From All-That-Is comes finiteness, but this is borne from the infinite
And when the finiteness is complete, the infinite remains.

From this One, All-That-Is, comes form and manifestation,
Only to reveal its formlessness and invisibility at its source.
From this One, All-That-Is, comes suffering,
But it comes so that you may know the joy and pure love behind it.

This All-That-Is can be the many and the One.
Even with the millions and billions, it is still the One.
The infinite splitting of itself is purely to experience the love infinitely and then return to the One.
Amazingly, this whole All-That-Is experience is about experiencing love in its most fundamental form.

Therefore, all of creation, even the dark, the endings, the suffering,
Have love at the heart of it.
So that the One, All-That-Is, can know its Self from infinite perspectives
And return unto itself.

This love that we refer to can also be known as God.
A pureness of love that manifests in a myriad of forms but with the simplest of essences.
Another way to put it is that God is the feeling of love,
And love is the feeling of God.

You, dear Human, are part of that interplay:
From love. Of love; Moving into love and experiencing love in all its forms,
Through your journey in life.
Even those things not so pleasing to you:
The dark, the endings and the suffering are all borne out of love.
So that You and the one you may refer to as God can know light, love and union more completely.
So that You may return to this understanding from newer, unique angles,
Borne out of life's tribulations.

Knowing this: The start and end position of love,
Its journey, its evolution and the myriad forms and representations it uses as its vehicles.
And knowing the reason for love,
Gives You a foundation for understanding yourself and your life in terms of vibration.

For vibration is your indicator and reminder of the non-physical realm
That you are part of with your I AM Self.

## Experience Life Beyond the Seen and Heard

Imagine you had no eyes; what would you use to inform yourself about the world around you?
How would you gather information about the world?
Of course, you would use your other senses,
But let's further suppose you also couldn't hear.
You would then be more connected with the feelings inside you,
More connected with the vibration of things,
How they made you feel, and your responses to them and the world around you.

This sense would be non-physical, based on energetic feedback,
Based on vibration.
You would sense your surroundings,
And the feelings they invoke would provide feedback
On how pleasing those experiences might be.

The degree to which they make you feel good
Would indicate your alignment, resonance, or compatibility with the things around you.
You would be living and practising according to the Laws of cause-and-effect or attraction.
Then, you would exercise your free will as a human being,
And consciously pursue a better feeling experience,
Based on the reliable system of vibration, cause-and-effect, or the law of attraction.

The better you got at 'vibration-interpretation' over time,
The better you would become at choosing good-feeling experiences.
This is what we are asking you to do:
To develop your interpretation of energy and vibration.

Of course, this will be harder for you at first
If you do have all your physical senses in working order,
Because for most of you, they may be your dominant senses.
However, this sense exists for you anyway, and believe it or not,
It is your natural and primary sense.

This vibration-interpretation sense is your authentic connection to everything possible.
It's your lifeline to all that exists,
Your connection to God,
The gateway to all you will experience,
And the *feeling* and flow of love in your life.

The better you get at vibration interpretation,
The more you will orient your life experience according to vibration.
When you begin to discern how things feel energetically and vibrationally,
You will become better at knowing when things feel better and when things feel worse.

When you do this, you will feel empowered,
Able to embrace and participate more knowingly
In your physical experience of All-That-Is.

## Visualise Your Higher Vibration Journey

Imagine again that you cannot hear or see,
And must navigate the world solely based on the vibrations you feel.
Instead of noticing limitations around you,
You'd be guided by positive experiences,
Making choices based on how they feel,
Regardless of their appearances or perceived benefits.

You would consciously opt out of things that didn't feel good.
Now, imagine living life hopping from one good feeling to another,
Your life becoming an unending hop-to-hop of *'being'* that just felt good.
You would then know you were having a happy life.

As a consequence of frequent good feeling vibratory experience,
You would match and attract subsequent good feeling phenomena.
That would become your default vibrational level,
And you would notice your life getting better and better.

Imagine now, if you consciously sought even better feelings,
Attracting experiences of higher vibratory resonance,
Creating an even more joyful life.
This is something to ponder –
The endless possibilities of such a life.
That all of this is possible.

The physical world around you, with its buildings, cafés, and people,
All appear convincingly real.
Yet, these are all manifestations of vibration – energy, and love,
Accepted as real by many, for so long, forming a collective agreement of existence.
But remember, they are here, formed from energy and vibration,
Manifestations of collective energy – your energy.

The physical world, with its buses, cafés, and buildings
Serves you in the physical realm, providing a stage for exploration.
To move about, play, and explore while in your physical body.
These things exist to serve, not to dictate your reality.
They are the product of presupposed, pre-imagined vibrational creations,
Brought into being by collective vibration – your vibration.
But considering them as the ultimate representation of the world's existence is limiting.

Therefore, if you identify with them and adhere to assumptions
About why they exist and what limitations they present:
If you take these physical things in your world to be ultimately true,
And believe that the physical world is the only form of existence,
*You* become limited.

Allowing the physical manifestation to inform you of what you are,
Veils the Non-physical I AM to who you are.
It stunts your belief, understanding and acceptance in the Divine Self
And what you can expect to happen.

# Aligning Your Actions with Vibration

Now imagine integrating this approach with your abilities –
Seeing, hearing, tasting, touching and smelling.
In other words, you have a functioning set of physical sense organs,
Allowing you to navigate the time-space world, Planet Earth, with practicality.

You can catch a bus, order a meal in a restaurant,
Or arrive at a concert on time.
Yet, you still prioritise your internal vibrations,
Letting them guide your life decisions and actions.

You become primarily vibration-oriented,
Using your physical body to implement actions
Suggested by your feelings.
For instance, if something feels good, you move towards it,
Engage with it, and enjoy the feedback from the physical thing you interact with.

We believe this is the ideal blend –
A perfect union of the physical and non-physical experience.
We encourage this balance because it facilitates interaction for you
As a non-physical being inhabiting a physical body
In a physical, time-space world.

We wish to guide you towards living this way,
Encouraging your best way to exist as a human being –
The perfect manifestation of physical reality,
All while maintaining super-conscious being-ness
In the non-physical realm, existing from love,
As a facet of God, of infinite being-ness.

## Your Passage to Mastery

We know, of course, that part of what it means
To be Human, in your temporary expression,
Is that it can be challenging at times to remember this.
Sometimes, you may forget the relationship
Between the physical and non-physical You,
And the connection via vibration,
Because the existing physical world is so amazing and convincing!

The physical world around you is distracting,
And can become your dominant informant about what is real.
If you let go of the I AM Self (temporarily),
The full radiance of the physical world is so stunning
That you can live and create in it tangibly.

There is a phrase: "God is in the detail,"
And this is true because this detail is microscopic when scrutinised.
Allowing your participation in it at every level
Of physical and mental necessity.

However, the art of living as a Human being
Is to blend the experience of both physical and non-physical being-ness:
To keep the relationship in *'living practice'*
To that which is the foundation of you:
Energy, Love, God.

Perhaps you are disturbed by the word 'God',
In which case, may we suggest you change the word to 'source'.
Remember that 'God' as a word has become manifest,
Yet it is the source of All-That-Is!
It is both manifest and unmanifest.

Therefore, it is limiting its essence
By attempting to define it with a word!
However, God is all words, and all words are God.
All things are God.
It can also be considered as:
The Source, The Universe, The Divine,
The Infinite, The All-That-Is, The Eternal,
The Supreme Energy, The Cosmic Intelligence,
And The Universal Consciousness.
There are many more names for God, too.

We would like you to feel free
To use whichever term resonates with you,
And aligns best with your feelings.
The goal is to acknowledge and connect with
The greater energy that permeates all existence.

With this as your path, recognise living
As an artful, evolutionary, joyful experience.
An experience where you *aim* to feel good,
You *aim* to feel love.
You know the great I AM that you are.
You embody the two Selves in tandem.

Therefore, keep the understanding and connection
To Your non-physical essence, which is vibration-based,
As a tool for the physical You,
To read the quality of your encounters and phenomena before you.
Hold this *connection* first and foremost.

Keep this connection so that you do not lose sight
Of yourself and who you really are.
Keep this connection so you do not deny your light, capability, or worthiness.
Where *everything* is possible;
You are infinite (beyond this physical life) and surrounded by unconditional love.

You have come forward to embrace the physicalness of life
And everything to experience and sense within it.
There is incredible joy to be had when you master the art
Of letting the vibration of what you feel, first and foremost,
Lead the way to what you choose to experience...

Follow the positive feeling of an idea,
Let it guide whether you embrace and act upon it.
Feel the *'being'* and connection, let these inform your actions.
Life will then transform into an exciting, passionate journey;
Interesting, satisfying, constantly evolving,
Creative, expansive, integrated,
Filled with joy and authenticity.
Live like this, and you will soar!

## Grant Your Inner Divinity

Know: You have stepped down vibrationally
Into the physicality of life and everything you can experience and sense within it.
There is a density to this physical life that you lead,
For you are energy become matter.
But as manifest physicality, you experience the joy of action
In conjunction with the non-physical aspect of I AM.
Thus, you can co-create amongst the seemingly solid matter of your planet
And with the other Beings on it:
With all the joy, texture, and sensation that accompanies it.

There is immense enjoyment when you can weave your divinity into the physical realm,
When you can channel your divine energy through your Human intellect,
When you can master the art of allowing the vibration of what you feel,
Prioritising this to inform your choice of experience.

By consciously choosing what to feel:
Following the good feeling of an idea –
An indication to you that you should participate in it and act on it:
Feel the Being-ness in the present moment as your informant for doing.
You are then Being vibration-oriented and using vibration
As your precursor, as your connection to Self,
To steer you towards your most rewarding actions.

This is different to being 'action-oriented',
Which does not originate from Self-connection.
Instead, action-orientation originates from non-present data information,
From copying and repeating what others do and what you believe should be done.
It stems from over-identification with the physical world,
And does not always bring you the experience
That is in alignment with Who-You-Really-Are.

Stay in the moment, *everything* exists within the now.

CHAPTER 2

# Energy

## The Spectrum of Creation

## The Universal Thread

We wish to talk about energy from a metaphysical perspective
As an endless flow or a universal constant.
We would like you to think of it as a pervasive and infinite force flowing through all existence,
Where every fragment, no matter how minute, mirrors the divine.

Throughout the vast and infinite realms of creation
There is but one energy.
And that energy we all share –
You, and all other forms of being.
That is because energy is an infinite force that is all-pervasive,
Moving through all forms of existence,
Enabling experiences and perspectives.

## Divine Consciousness Within Energy's Flow

Energy is a vehicle of consciousness.
And this consciousness is God.
We have mentioned that love and God are the basis and foundation of all that exists.

However, energy can be thought of as the dynamic expression of this underlying reality,
Because moving through different forms, experiences, and consciousness,
Energy provides endless expression of All-That-Is.

It gains infinite viewpoints and focus for God.
So that love can experience itself.
So that God can experience itself.
Shapes, forms, realms, levels.
All are equal in value.
All part of the same whole.

## The Holographic Principle

Every part of existence in all creation, manifest and unmanifest, is holographic.

Just as a hologram contains the entire image, no matter how small,
Every aspect of existence, down to the smallest particle,
Contains within it the entirety of the divine consciousness or God.

For example, consider a holographic picture of a tree.
If you cut that picture into smaller pieces,
Each piece would still contain a smaller but complete image of the tree.
Similarly, the entire cosmos exists within each part of the Universe,
No matter how seemingly insignificant.
We want to emphasise that God, or divine consciousness,
Is not separate from creation and all forms of Being-ness within it,
But interwoven into every aspect of it.

Despite this infinity of form and creation,
There is simplicity and purity.
God exists within everything and everyone,
And in turn, everything and everyone exists within it.
It is, and we are, a continuous, interconnected cycle,
Where all creation and experience is an expression of God
And contains God within itself.
Everything is interconnected, equal in value, and a unique perspective of All-That-Is.

The expression: "holographic in nature"
May help you remember or accept all things' profound unity and interconnectedness.
The smallest particle or seemingly unimportant life form
Holds the blueprint of the entire Universe, creation, God, and All-That-Is.
Essentially, we would like you to understand that God is not an external entity,
But the core essence of all existence.
This is what is meant by "the All existing in the All."
Even if this is not apparent to you in your daily life,
You are here, worthy, Divine, whole, perfect, and part of All-That-Is.

We would like to convince you of Your inseparability from God!
You are an expression of God that embodies a unique consciousness perspective
That you have come to identify with in this life as:
Your name, personality, appearance, and so much more.

Yet this perspective is simply a unique facet of the whole;
The whole exists within you and around you simultaneously.
Your experience, therefore, is perfect,
Even if sometimes your life may not feel perfect to you.
For it cannot be anything else.

## Your Life-Force and Reality

In its most fundamental sense, energy is the potential to initiate movement,
Organise, change, and transform.
Energy is the medium through which God's consciousness is expressed in your physical world.
Therefore, every aspect of it contains the entirety of divine consciousness.

Energy can neither be created nor destroyed,
Only transformed from one form to another.
It is all-pervasive and infinite – the qualities of God.
Applying this understanding to your life as a Human,
Energy can be seen as the dynamic, active aspect of existence,
The driving force behind all change, transformation, and expression.

You are the Individual of God in a uniquely-expressed physical Human Being form,
Allowing energy, the dynamic expression of the Divine, to flow through you.
This divine energy is believed to be present in all things,
Giving life, consciousness, and movement.
It is the animating force that drives the Universe,
The catalyst for change, growth, and evolution.
This divine energy is also perceived as infinite, boundless, and eternal.

# Resonance and Shared Creation

Therefore, understanding energy in first principles and concerning God
Brings us to a deeper realisation of the interconnectedness and unity of all things.
It implies that all existence is a dynamic, ever-changing divine energy,
Continually expressing, transforming, and experiencing itself in infinite forms.

Know, therefore, that there is a wholeness and a perfection
To that which you are expressing.
For the mastery that flows through everything
Is already perfection, wholesome, unified
And wanting for nothing outside of itself.
Because there is nothing outside of itself.
Affirming this, affirming who you are and why you are here,
Will allow you to come to terms with this.

Somewhere in you, you may feel this.
Somewhere in you, you may accept this.
Within you, you know this.

Recognise this in every expression of life around you,
Then your understanding of Who-You-Really-Are
And who we are, and how love is,
Will dramatically shift your life's format and quality.

It could also make your experience of cause-and-effect, or the law of attraction,
Much more tangible and noticeable.

You perceive cause-and-effect as a linear sequence of events that occur separately in time
and space...
In your life and in your world.
Your perception is observed in the three-dimensional reality you inhabit.

However, when you begin to comprehend that God's Energy permeates all of existence,
You also realise that this energy is not bound by the limitations of time and space
As you understand and relate to them in your life.
Instead, it is omnipresent and omnipotent,
Simultaneously existing in all places and times.

In understanding this, the concept of cause-and-effect
Takes on a more immediate and intimate meaning
As it is no longer about something happening now that will cause an effect later
(although you can still perceive it that way);
Rather, it is a dynamic, ever-present interplay of energies
That are constantly influencing you and being influenced by you.

## Divine Energy into the Mundane

This understanding may take some getting used to.
It may take a few reminders.
However, this will dramatically shift your perception of life.
And remembering this intimate connection to God and everything around you
Will empower you to recognise that your thoughts, emotions, and actions
Are personally and universally impactful.

Recognise that your intentions, beliefs, and actions,
Sent out into the world,
Immediately affect not just your surroundings but also yourself.
This is because we are all interconnected parts
Of a unified field of Divine Energy.

Therefore, we would like you to be inspired
To consciously engage with life, knowing that you are co-creators
In this universal flow of energy.
Where you will understand that your power to effect change is not limited to your immediate surroundings,
But extends to the broader Universe.

By aligning your intentions with love and with Who-You-Really-Are,
Your energy can create ripples of positive change that reverberate through your life,
Improving, not only your personal life but also your world and other Beings.

By understanding this profound connection,
You realise that you are active participants in the divine unfolding of creation,
And by remembering your true nature, you understand
That you are Divine beings having a human experience,
Capable of shaping your reality through the energy you choose to embody and express.
Capable of shifting your Being-ness into a vibration-oriented experience,
Because vibration is the mechanism through which Divine Energy is expressed.

All forms of existence are composed of God's energy,
Constantly vibrating at different frequencies.

This God energy includes your thoughts, emotions, and physical bodies.
These all create different energetic vibrations.
This principle is based on the understanding that like attracts like.
Therefore, your vibrational frequency influences the events, circumstances,
And people you attract into your life.

Being vibration-oriented means consciously and deliberately feeling your vibrations.
This is done by feeling your emotions and then choosing your action,
Based on those feelings.
By aligning your thoughts, emotions, and actions to better-feeling things
With the higher vibrations of love and joy,
You can deliberately and consciously shape your life.

You can pull in and deliberately attract things
That feel better for you by allowing how things make you feel,
To inform you of the thoughts, feelings, and actions you take in your world.
This is about becoming aware of your internal state
By doing this, you attract positive experiences into your lives.
It brings abundant flow to you from all directions.

By understanding this, you become more conscious of cause-and-effect
And, ultimately, the impact of your feelings and your energy.
You also align yourself with Who-You-Really-Are.
This is because the essence of God is within you.
God is love, which is the highest vibration.
By resonating with this frequency, you attune yourself
To the divine essence within and around you.
This connection facilitates a greater sense of Oneness,
Expands your consciousness and enhances your ability to manifest your desires.

## Attuning with Elevated Frequencies

Suppose you were to truly integrate this understanding
And become consciously vibration-oriented in your life,
Aligning your thoughts, emotions, and actions with the higher frequencies of Divine Energy.
In that case, you open yourself up to transcend the limitations of the third-dimensional reality,
Specifically, the time-space parameters of cause-and-effect.
This is because the connection between cause-and-effect
Becomes more direct at these higher vibrational frequencies.
You would start to experience a higher consciousness,
Where manifestation can occur instantaneously,
And the linear constraints of time and space are less rigid.

Essentially, you would move into a state of Being
Where you exist in harmony with the non-physical aspect of who you are,
Effortlessly co-creating your reality in alignment with your highest good.

Indeed, understanding that you are an *energy* Being,
And that this is an expression of love implies that we are all perfectly interconnected.
Regardless of the *form* or *frequency* of energy,
Whether you perceive it as good or bad, each energy expression originates from a place of wholeness, love, God-ness,
Or the original Source, All-That-Is.

Each form has the unifying essence of All-That-Is,
Signifying that the energy source is one, yet in varying forms of a perfect whole.
As you engage with these words, allow your shoulders to relax
With the understanding of this teaching.

Understand that there is no judgment.
There are no good or bad definitions.
There is no wrong path.
You are energy; you are love.
You are God; we are in union.

Our conversation is part of the wholeness,
The perfectness of being.
It is a match of frequency, of vibration,
And an illustration of attraction.
All are mechanisms of movement,
And expressions of the same Oneness.

The fact that you've come across this teaching is no coincidence.
For you haven't stumbled upon it.
Can you see that?
This reading experience is a vibrational match
To something you have created within your life journey
That has drawn this moment towards you.

We would like you to know that you are this energy.
And we are this energy.
And here is where we meet.
We acknowledge your true essence.
You are everything, and everything is you.
We are merely different expressions of you and you of us.
Love forms the foundation of it all.

Accepting this, feeling it, living it,
And integrating this understanding into your life,
Can completely shift its format and bring limitless joy to you!
We hope you can feel the thrill, even by contemplating the prospect of it.

Therefore, consciously engage with life.
Come towards everything with love.
Approach everything you see with love and recognition of the energy we belong to and are part of.
Feel the energy of different things as an expression of uniqueness and of God.
Explore the joy of love.

Even in the unfolding of less pleasant experience that comes your way,
Whether in physical or non-physical form, know it has love at its core
And will help you choose a better vibrational experience
With higher expressions of energy.

CHAPTER 3

# Transmission

## An Invocation to Conscious Living

# Divine Simplicity

Embarking on the vibrational nature of life can seem new and unusual.
Let's EMBRACE the simplicity of your vibrational existence,
A journey both intricate and straightforward,
Yoking together your physical and non-physical self.

We want you to know how easy it is once you understand
The nature of creation and Your Divine Self.
In the vast expanse of your reality and the world around you,
Where every visible and invisible thing is powered by energy,
You navigate through a sea of vibrations,
Each one a unique expression and carrier of God energy.

Because all energy is vibration,
And vibration is a way for creation to organise itself.

Envision your energy as a pebble gently cascading into a serene pond,
Creating ripples that reverberate throughout the Universe around you.
How do the ripples your energy creates interact with the world around you?
The reality you experience is a perfect synthesis of this.

Now, picture each being as a pebble,
Their thoughts, emotions, and actions sending ripples through the Universe,
Intertwining with your own and the universal energies around them.
Every entity within all of creation, including your human self,
Emits a unique frequency, harmonising and interacting with the entirety of creation.

Everything within creation emits and mirrors these vibrations,
Expressing themselves through unique frequencies.

We wish to talk about energy from a metaphysical perspective
As an endless flow or a universal constant.
We would like you to think of it as a pervasive and infinite force flowing through all existence,
Where every fragment, no matter how minute, mirrors the divine.

Throughout the vast and infinite realms of creation
There is but one energy.
And that energy we all share –
You, and all other forms of being.
That is because energy is an infinite force that is all-pervasive,
Moving through all forms of existence,
Enabling experiences and perspectives.

## Seeing Your Reflection

Your emotions are a sensitive barometer for the energy around you.
They are your Guide.
Higher frequencies elevate your feelings.
Lower ones offer lower feelings.

You are in a continuous transmission and reception of energy!
Engaged in a relationship with All-That-Is, which mirrors your vibrational output.
Transmit a specific vibration, and it will resonate back to you by the Universe.

You'll receive it because you will be in harmony with it.
Because like attracts like.
And resonance finds unity.

Therefore, immerse yourself fully as a vibrational being,
As a divine energy entity.
And witness the enhancement and synchronicity in your life,
Where the gap between cause-and-effect in your physical world diminishes.

In your temporal and spatial world,
You experience a delay between the frequencies you transmit
And those that bounce back to you.

That's because in the realm you are embodied within,
Things appear to happen sequentially,
As if they happen over a period of time and in different places.

Nevertheless, what you transmit is always reflected to you without exception.
But as powerful divine beings, you possess the capability
To influence your own frequencies,
By consciously choosing your thoughts, feelings, and actions.

Positive thoughts and actions emit higher frequencies,
While their negative counterparts emit lower ones.
For example, when frustration sets in,
You are broadcasting a lower frequency to the Universe,
Which will inevitably mirror back to you.

Recognising these lower frequencies as they arise
Grants you the power to shift your experiences away from unpleasantness
And towards a higher vibrational state.
This is the practice of conscious living.

You can deliberately control your vibrational output
To enhance your life experience.
We encourage you to remember this in your day-to-day life
And to be *vibration-oriented*.
Therefore, choose actions based on their feelings.
Doing so elevates your vibrational output, which will be mirrored back to you,
Rather than doing something that might not feel good, consequently sending out a lower frequency.

## Finding Your True North

Equally, we would like to point out that if you are not feeling good,
Take note and use the helpful internal indicator (your emotions)
To help you *feel* your way back to a better place.
If you will, this internal indicator is like an *inner compass*
That shows you where your *true north* is by feeling good.
What we mean by *true north* is the feeling of alignment and harmony within yourself.

When you're off course;
When your vibrational state is not aligned with your inherent signature energy
Or your natural feeling of well-being,
You'll notice a decline in the frequency of your vibratory output.

What we describe is an impeccable internal system –
An internal indicator that directs you back towards unity, wholeness,
And the profound connection of love that encompasses all.
It serves as the bridge to Who-You-Really-Are:
Your bridge between non-physical and physical.

Your non-physical internal system is the range of feelings and emotions you feel.
Within yourself, you can experience the whole gamut of human emotions:
From the lowest frequency of energy to the highest,
From the most negative, contracted, dark, limited feelings
Of despair, depression, and anger
To the most positive, expansive, light, and limitless feelings of joy.

# Practising Conscious Living

Practising conscious living involves deliberately controlling
Your vibrational output so that you can enhance your life experiences
And enhance your life in general.

Despite the distractions of the physical senses in your physical life,
Your internal indicator is effortlessly accessible and understandable.
It is a link to the non-physical aspect of You.
It has always been there, and it will always be there.
It is eternal and outreaches the limits of your physical body.
This is your truest gauge of what's good or bad for you.
And it's your most reliable guide to happiness and fulfilment in your physical life.

We would like you to know this, and we would like you to remember this
In your day-to-day thoughts, feelings and actions.
This may be a new way of going about things in your daily life,
And challenging to remember at first.

However, even just remembering this way of being from time to time
Will be effective for you and will change your energy.
The more you remember this way and consciously try to implement it,
The more your energy and life will change positively!

We would like to remind you to be vibration-oriented first and foremost
So that you can consciously choose your physical actions
Based on how they feel, and consciously choose your energy transmission.

Maintain alignment with your true joyful, light, expansive and limitless nature.
Uphold your physical life with your non-physical I AM presence!
Weave your sense of this non-physical energy into your physical life.

CHAPTER 4

# Channeling-Connecting

**Bringing Non-Physical into Physical**

# What is Channeling?

Embark on a journey of conscious connection in your life.
For all of creation is about connection,
All of creation is in a relationship with itself!
And love is the force that propels all energy to seek resonance and unity.

Connection feels good to you, dear human,
Because it is the confirmation that unity is the truth:
We are all one and part of the same Whole.
Therefore, seek connection to each other and the things that make you feel good.

The word *Channeling* refers to the process of drawing broader energy
And consciousness into your individual intellect.
Channeling connects individuals to the non-physical aspects
Of union and the I AM Self.

This connection enables the enlightenment and wisdom
Of All-That-Is to permeate into Your physical reality.
When you channel, you effortlessly merge your consciousness
With the broader experience of I AM Self and other perspectives of Being or God,
Allowing this consciousness to resonate through your thoughts, ideas, and perceptions.

Amazingly, it is an effortless pathway to connect to the non-physical aspects of Union and Yourself.

Channeling higher consciousness illuminates You!
Inspiration, insight, perspective, and truth are all available to you in higher states,
As well as deep peace, love, and joy.

A deeper connection to Yourself, your higher vibrational I AM Self, enables you
To bring forth the enlightened understanding and wisdom of the whole
Into your physical reality, thereby enriching your physical experience.

## Seeking Positive Resonance

If you aspire to consciously align with higher consciousness and more uplifting experiences,
Understanding that this connection is contingent upon the vibration you emit,
Is paramount.

We encourage you to refine the skill of elevating your vibration,
Becoming more attuned to lifting your vibrational state,
And trusting your feelings, which are always a reliable indicator
Of what you are transmitting,
Because the connection to higher consciousness depends on the vibration
Transmitted by the individual.
Uplifting experiences result from a higher vibrational state
And better feeling thoughts.

Uplifting experiences come from higher consciousness in your physical life.
If you make your quest to find good feelings and emotions a priority in your life,
You will enhance your life's joy and fulfilment;
And strengthen your belief that what you emit vibrationally
Is what you'll attract.

If you intend to access elevated realms of consciousness
Or broader experiential perspectives,
Increasing your vibrational frequency will enable you
To match and resonate with experiences of a similar vibrational value.

What experiences, wisdom, and connections might unfold before you
As you navigate through the harmonious alignment of your being
With the higher frequencies of All-That-Is?

As with everything in creation, there is an energy exchange
That aligns with your frequency, like a data exchange.

In your pursuit to have a consciousness exchange
With frequencies that soar higher and higher, you are attempting
To match that frequency.

Throughout your physical life experience,
You carry a vibrational pattern denser than non-physical phenomena.
Yet, we still encourage you to elevate your vibration
And find a higher consciousness
To illuminate your life and light up those around you!

# Channeling Light

Ponder for a moment that your consciousness is like a luminous bulb
In the vast darkness of what is unknown or unapparent in your physical world.
As you elevate your consciousness, your light intensifies,
Reaching farther and wider, illuminating previously unseen possibilities
And connections in the expansive universal consciousness.
Your light, your vibrational energy, becomes harmonious
With the things you want in your life, and you begin to see more around you,
Becoming more enlightened and able to share your light with those around you.

For some of you, it may be possible to match your frequency
With that of other conscious beings, finding a resonance
That enables you to harmonise your vibrational transmissions.
This alignment allows a data exchange or a consciousness exchange
Between you and the other.

This exchange is not necessarily about propelling your energy
Across the vastness of time and space, journeying through clouds and stars.
Instead, it's about harmonic alignment,
Wherein you automatically tune into the same frequency of consciousness, and data, or information,
And energy becomes shared and accessible to both parties in unison.

In your physical lives on Earth, you are already experiencing this data exchange,
As the non-physical communication exchange is perpetually present,
Explaining why you can sometimes feel a connection to other beings or creatures
Without the necessity of words and physical action.

## A Living Bridge

Channeling and connecting is akin to becoming a living bridge
Between the boundless energies of the Universe and of God
And the focused power of your individual intellect.
In this process, you're inviting a broader consciousness
Than what you are aware of in your daily life
To infuse your thought processes and illuminate your understanding.
This is not a one-way street but a blend,
An integration of consciousness that offers new perspectives and insights.

Channeling and connecting is about aligning with Who-You-Really-Are,
Allowing it to permeate your being and enrich your physical life on Earth.

Nurture your connection to your I AM Self:
Unify and integrate this into your physical Self.
Nurture all connections that make you feel good.
Raise your consciousness so that you may evolve towards complete freedom and joy!
Consider this the *marriage* of the human Self and your divine Self!

CHAPTER 5

# Resonance

## Dispelling the Illusion of Separation

## The Invisible Pull

You are a divine being, a being of resonance,
Living in a Universe where everything vibrates in response to everything else.
This vibration, the foundation of All-That-Is, is integral to your life,
To how you came to be in this physical body, to how you see your world.
You are non-physical in nature, yet experience in a physical realm
Where things *appear* solid but are actually only vibrations resonating,
Creating the illusion of solidity in a space that's mostly empty.

Resonance occurs in your human body and conscious mind.
Your organs, thoughts, words, and behaviours have their own frequencies.
How does resonance feel, you may ask?

Divine One, your experience of resonance can be physical, emotional, harmonious, amplifying.
Your body, thoughts or emotions vibrate in synchronicity with what you respond to.
You may feel it as a sensation, find it pleasant or joyful.
You may feel a sense of connection, understanding, or empathy,
Where your thoughts and feelings grow stronger, fuller, richer.
You become more receptive to what you resonate with
And can perceive and understand its reality more deeply.
Resonance creates a feeling of balance and well-being in your life.

## Awakening Your Awareness

It powerfully bridges gaps between seemingly disparate elements,
Yet, in truth, nothing is disparate. Everything originates from the one.

Resonating with people, groups, animals, and higher vibratory consciousness manifests as
*Empathy, understanding, alignment, deep connection.*
When you connect or resonate with another consciousness,
You share energy, information, understanding.

You may not perceive it with your physical senses,
But this transactional relationship with All-That-Is is fundamental to your life's progression,
Shared experiences, collective wisdom and evolution of your species.
Resonance is *always* happening and guides you to things that feel good.

While you will have experienced resonance many times,
We encourage you to actively seek it out.
Awareness of what you resonate with is a helpful guide for your life path.
Embrace it, and enjoy the positive feelings that accompany it.

Upon meeting someone, have you felt that you've known them forever?
That is resonance.

There is no end to the vastness of consciousness!
To resonate on a more expanded scale with higher forms of consciousness,
You will need to raise your consciousness to a higher frequency.
Here lie deep insight, wisdom, and spiritual revelation –
Revelations that come from beyond usual thoughts and senses.

You may notice these revelations that come from beyond your usual thoughts and senses.
Your I AM Self *is* higher consciousness, the funnel of intuition, non-local consciousness,
And multi-dimensional experiences like telepathy.
Perceptions like these can provide temporary detachment from your ego and the physical world.

Raising your consciousness yields a powerful, joyful, transformative experience.
It attunes you vibrationally to higher ways of being, progression, and enlightenment.
If more individuals have perceptions like these, humanity will evolve more quickly.

*How can you apply this practically in daily life?*
Seek to connect with everything that feels good!
Doing so will raise your consciousness,
And will enable you to deeply understand the interconnectedness of all things.
Actively look for and attune to positive, life-affirming, love-centred experiences!
This will elevate the quality of your life, its encounters, and relationships.

Finding resonance is finding harmony with your world, all Beings, and your divinity.
It is the universal language of connection, love, unity.

Allow your divine I AM consciousness to stream through your body.
Revel in these binary qualities of Self in harmony.
This is the highest way to live your life.

Whatever you experience is part of the greatest love that God has for You.
It is the pathway of God's energy:
To follow resonance is your divine, unique expression through physical life,
Lighting up as cues that you are going the right way.

CHAPTER

6

# Imagination is Key

## The Boundless Realm

Imagination is vital to your understanding of non-physical experience.
Without it, visualising becomes impossible.

Visualising non-physical experiences helps you navigate the non-physical realm.
By *non-physical realm,* we refer to a domain beyond the bandwidth and limitations of your physical world.
This realm encompasses dimensions of conscious energy,
Unconstricted by time and space,
With a broader perspective of All-That-Is.

Your imagination plays a crucial role in your relationship with the non-physical realm,
Accessing, exploring, and interacting with these dimensions of consciousness
Through your imaginative faculties.

There's a paradox here. You may question the reality of your imagination,
Thinking, *This isn't real; I'm just making it up.*
Because what you see in your imagination is not solid.
Yet, what you see in life is also not solid!
What you think of as *making it up* isn't quite so.

The process referred to as 'making it up' is channeling,
Or drawing into your mind information corresponding to your resonating frequency.
Sensations, feelings, ideas, thoughts, and images that come via imagination
Are part of All-That-Is, not emerging from nowhere.
Because *everything* that exists is part of All-That-Is.

The non-physical world is frequency- and vibration-based,
Just like your physical world.
Therefore, all forms, physical or non-physical, derive from this.

# Transcending Physical Limitations

Divine One, your imagination is a powerful, intuitive transducer,
Allowing perception of realities beyond your physical senses.
When you *imagine*, you are not just creating fantasies.
You're tuning into a different level of perception and reality,
Converting abstract, inspirational and creative energy into tangible ideas, and visions.
So, even if it feels like you are making it up,
It does not mean it isn't accurate or meaningful.

What you experience through imagination is intuitive perception,
Sensing and exploring the non-physical realm,
Connecting and translating the limitless, ethereal realm into your physical reality.
Trust this process.
Let your imagination carry you to a broader consciousness.

Therefore, images and forms received in imagination operate under frequency,
Attraction and resonance principles.
Honour the vibratory stream resonating through your imagination;
It is woven into the fabric of your consciousness.

Imagination is your vehicle for unique expression,
Channeling divine energy into your physical Being.

## The Vibration of What You Imagine

Non-physical experiences in imagination take many forms,
Some ineffable, beyond the description of language.
While you may find them difficult to articulate or qualify, tune in to how they feel.
Let them guide you to higher-frequency consciousness.
Remember, you are free to choose and change your experiences,
In your quest to aligning with what feels best.

*What if you experience another form of consciousness that is not human?*

Should you establish contact with a non-human being,
Doubt often follows about the encounter's validity.
Such scepticism represents a healthy dialogue between physical self and expanding consciousness.
Over time, developing confidence in imaginative experiences,
And understanding the non-solid nature of everything that exists,
You'll learn to recognise these experiences as guidance
Towards broader consciousness and personal growth.

Tuning into higher consciousness breaks down barriers of doubt and fear,
Making your perception more fluid and able to discern truth.
Experiencing higher conscious beings enlightens and progresses your life.
Consider them guideposts towards greater enlightenment.

If you experience contact with another consciousness form,
Your imagination may present recognisable aspects –
A shape, a face, a pattern, a colour –
Assisting in processing and integrating the experience physically,
In a way that your mind can comprehend.

Understand that the ultimate expression of love underlies these experiences,
Regardless of their form.
Sometimes jostling your physical senses,
Appearing as something completely new to you,
Prodding the expression of your consciousness,
Encouraging your questioning, analysis, integration, and growth.
Or may take on a form that triggers a fearful response from you.

## Deciphering Divine Intelligence

There is nothing to fear when you realise that you are God-In-Form,
And are part of the *same energy* that also produces the trigger of your fear.
Reflect on this: Forms presenting via imagination are agents of enlightenment,
Paving your life path through physical experience.
You are a pathway of God-expression.
Everything in the Universe, all forms of Being-ness you encounter, is God-In-Action,
In an all-encompassing union of experiencing itself.

Embrace your imagination; when allowed, it enables intuitive knowing,
Streaming together both physical and non-physical aspects of yourself,
Perceiving beyond the five senses,
Guiding towards connectivity, creativity, and contentment.

Imagination activates your passion, motivation, ambition,
Bringing profound insight through vivid imagery and sensations.
Trust this process.
Remember that your imagination navigates the expansive world of non-physical experiences,
Envisioning realities beyond current circumstances.
Thus, your imagination is the bearer of celestial illumination.

CHAPTER

7

# Connection and Making Contact

## Whispers Through the Celestial Veil

## Adjusting to the Brightness of Higher Consciousness

*Connection* is one way to describe the sharing of vibration or resonance
With another being in the larger field of consciousness of All-That-Is.

Imagine *harmonising*.

In this kind of connection or contact,
You are liaising in the same vibrational space,
Harmonised into the same frequency,
Just like more than one listener tuning into the same radio station,
Where all who tune into that frequency can access the same information or song.
This is what happens when you have made contact with another being.

Now, contact can be as fleeting as the beat of a butterfly wing,
Over and then gone, leaving the sense that this has just happened.
Or it can be longer,
Especially the more used to the sense you become
And the more acclimatised to the energy and frequency you are.

We say *energy*, for you may feel the difference in energy type
Between you and the Being you encounter.
We say *frequency*, because your frequency would have raised higher than usual
To meet with and match the frequency that the other Being can accommodate
To establish contact with you.

What we would like you to understand
Is that this is something that can happen to greater or lesser degrees.
You will always be in control of it,
As you are always in control of your own will, thoughts, and energy.

Contact or the feeling that you have connected with another being
May feel like your imagination at first.
This is where we ask you to remember
How important it is to validate what you get through your imagination.
It is the gateway or portal to read and translate frequency
Into tangible forms your cognitive mind can understand or at least relate to.
It bridges the non-physical realm and the ordinary working human mind.

Imagination can synthesise all sorts of forms, symbols, archetypes, shapes, and experiences
That the human mind can recognise from its archives of living and experience
So that higher frequency and higher concepts can be translatable,
Even if they remain somewhat cryptic.
And when they do, this allows time for integration into the normal psyche.

Although contact may be brief and momentary,
You may have accompanying reactions.
As we have mentioned, this may be difficult for you to acclimatise to,
And you may feel overwhelmed, unbalanced, tired, over-stimulated or fearful.

That's because when you consciously connect to higher frequencies of consciousness,
It's like you're inviting a much stronger, brighter light into your system.
This can cause a temporary over-stimulation
As your body and consciousness try to assimilate and adjust to this higher energy.

There is nothing for you to endure if it makes you feel out of sorts.
Therefore, when these sensations occur,
Pause. Come out of your place of connection.
Take a drink, a nap; walk in nature, or have a conversation with a loved one.
These things can connect you to your ordinary, awake, Earth-world state
And will rectify those feelings.
However, for some of you, you can fall into, or relax into, the experience.

For the most part, when acclimatised,
The experience of connection to wider consciousness in general and another being feels deeply peaceful, comforting, and present.
It feels this way because it is an experience of Union.
By 'Union', we mean that you have tapped into the more incredible feeling of what *you* are,
For all things share the same source or essence.

Here, we would like to say to you that there is no rush for anything;
No mission to accomplish,
No task to aim for, or goal to achieve,
Just the simple Being of Who-You-Really-Are
In resonance with other consciousness that has the same love at its core:
A unique perspective of God and All-That-Is.
Nothing more, and nothing less.
This resonance is a pure being-ness that is enough in itself.
Connection is deeply wonderful for any being as the pure awareness of the Greater Self
And Union is always there.

You remain the owner and master
Of both your physical and non-physical experience.
Though you can connect to consciousness that feels much bigger than you in your physical life,
You are still in control.
Even if you feel overwhelmed or over-stimulated,
You are still in control.
For you are a free-will being,
Able to break off the resonance and connection as you wish.
In all experiences, you have a choice.
Therefore, you can choose to disengage at any point.

Understand that you are the master controller
Of your experience and energy expression.
You have access to broader consciousness
And can channel your connection to it through your intellect and actions,
However you wish.
You can disengage your focus with anything that doesn't please you.
You are entirely supported in your physical body.
You are divine and equal to everything that exists within all creation.

We remind you that You are not alone
And are part of a much greater whole.
Your expansion and progression into new conscious experience
Is according to how you resonate.

## The Holistic View of Non-Physical Beings

In experiencing contact, you may feel a strong resonance with another Being.
In this case, you will feel a willingness to communicate.
This communication can come in many forms:
You can translate this consciousness into spoken or written words,
See visuals, or hear sounds.
You can translate this through creative expression.
You may receive data through your body,
And it is pleasant to be around you,
For you will have a healing energy that emanates from you.

All of you can channel this energy for healing to others!
You are always channeling energy into your physical world in these forms.
You are putting this energy exchange into action,
Which is the uniqueness of your particular energy stream,
Through your unique physical body-mind vehicle.

Understand that when a Being from the non-physical realm connects with you,
It reads your energy and understands you as a *whole*.
That is, from a *wholesome perspective*, you may not understand yourself.
For, in your physical world, you are habituated to knowing who you are
From your ego's point of view.

What we mean by your *ego's point of view*
Is your perspective of yourself based on your experiences in the physical world.
For example, how you look in the mirror,
What you think your personality is,
What you can recall about your life from memory;
Your personal data, societal conditioning, beliefs, and emotional attachments.
It is the story you have constructed about who you are and your place in the world,
Which is often limited and segmented.

However, when a higher consciousness Being from the non-physical realm connects with you,
They perceive you multidimensionally – from all perspectives.
They see beyond your narrow, ego-based view
To understand you entirely,
Including the aspects your ego may overlook or be unaware of.

Instead, this consciousness can understand and interpret your energy holistically,
Comprehending all aspects of your experience, mind, and psyche,
Physical and non-physical.
Furthermore, it is aware of you at all points in time
As there is no separation by time in non-physical experience.

Resonance is an automatic, instantaneous sharing of the same vibrational space.
This vibrational space is non-physical. (It is not really a space, but rather a consciousness).
Therefore, it gives access to all of You:
The You, which, from your perspective, may be veiled from *your* understanding.
These aspects that can be clear in the non-physical realm,
And not to your physical mind,
May include what is within your subconscious.

As unique human beings in the physical world,
You carry certain *blind spots* in your understanding of yourself and your consciousness.
These blind spots often include deeply-rooted fears, traumas, and belief systems
That you may not be fully aware of in your daily life.

As you learn to raise your consciousness –
By *raise your consciousness,* we mean elevate your energetic frequency –
You can gradually illuminate these hidden areas of your subconscious mind,
Leading to greater Self-awareness and integration.

The human psyche is adept at compartmentalising your experiences,
Which also applies to how you engage with non-physical phenomena.

Divine One, due to the complexity and expansive nature of all you experience,
Your mind must find ways to digest such experiences into comprehensible *bite-sized* pieces.
Your imagination plays a crucial role in this process.
It serves as a bridge between the known and the unknown,
The physical and the non-physical,
Rendering the unfathomable into something you can grasp and explore.

For example, when interacting with beings from the non-physical realm,
You often deal with consciousness that doesn't conform to your traditional constructs of form.
They may exist beyond the confines of the three-dimensional perception of your world,
Making it difficult for you to comprehend its true essence directly.

However, your imagination can translate these complex energetic patterns
Into something you can understand.
As we have said, it converts the abstract energy of non-physical being-ness
Into recognisable images, shapes, colours, patterns, faces, archetypes, and sensations.
Even if these symbols don't make immediate sense,
They can provide a tangible representation for your cognitive mind to process and explore.

Remember, these connections and contacts
Are agents for expanding your consciousness, and evolution, in the physical world.

# The Super-Natural Route and Your Healing Potential Within

If you have made contact
And are comfortable with this connection and feeling,
You can ask Yourself questions such as:
*How does this feel?* Or *How do I feel?*
Additionally, you can ask questions of the other, such as:
*Who are you?*

During this process, be patient and be at peace.
Take note of sensations, feelings or energy that move through you.
Your body works diligently to interpret data
For your cognitive mind to understand when this occurs.

However, your body and the cells within
May be processing the information in an *intangible* way for your mind to read,
Because the body perceives the energy differently.
In a sense, your mind speaks a different *language*
To that which the 'whole' of your body may understand.

Your mind interprets through the lens of your ego,
Your language, your conditioning and so forth.
While the rest of you and your body have a consciousness that is receiving *unfiltered,*
Until the mind sends its messages and its interpretations.
Fortunately, you have your imagination as a conduit!

However, with awareness and practice,
You can feel and perceive between the two: mind and body,
To gradually *integrate* your consciousness perception *holistically*.
Therefore, your patience
In allowing your physical apparatus to translate what it is picking up energetically, benefits you.

The range of experience you can perceive is infinite
Because it comes from the endless Oneness of All-That-Is,
Which is unified love: God.
You are that integral part of the experience:
You are *essential*, meaning *of its essence*.

Your physical experience is a Divine pathway,
And everything you encounter, in all of its range of feeling and vibration,
Is for the advancement of you as a Human Being.

In this regard, all encounters with all forms of consciousness
Act as the agent for your enlightenment.
For God is behind all of this.

We do not wish to dictate how the connection might happen for you
Because to do so could limit the unique experience that awaits you.
The experience is intangible to the ordinary human waking mind.
It is an energy experience with a place of understanding that is higher
Than what your mental faculties usually facilitate daily.

However, with your conscious presence in the here and now,
Your awareness of Who-You-Are and how you channel energy will develop.
We want you to know that greater understanding,
Awareness and embodiment of your I AM Self or God
Can offer immense transformation in your life.

This connection is an inherent part of the Universe;
It is the same vital force that allows flowers to bloom
And promotes healing within all living things.
By harnessing this energy within yourself,
You can stimulate profound physical, emotional, psychological, and subconscious healing.

This means you have within you the potential
To alleviate past pains, release heavy emotions,
And free yourself from feelings of loss, grief, anxiety, anger, greed, jealousy, and fear.

It also implies your ability to heal physical ailments, discomfort, and disease.
Yes, you are innately a healer!
This profound connection to All-That-Is
Is the core of who you are;
It is your reason for being,
Your ultimate ambition,
Your journey,
And your destination.

It encapsulates the entirety of your existence:
The beginning,
Middle,
And end.

It is an expression of boundless love, the embodiment of God.
It is how you contribute to the unity and oneness of all,
Serving life and its interconnectedness in your physical form.
This understanding and realisation are potent in moving through life,
Promoting healing, growth, and spiritual evolution.

We encourage you to remain open and conscious in your day-to-day life
As often as you can remember.
Always prioritise your vibration.

# Channeling

## Bringing the Celestial Down to Earth

Now, we would like to speak to you about channeling,
And what we mean by this.

It refers to the funneling of higher forms of consciousness
Into physical expressions, actions, or manifestations.

We would like to take this opportunity to clarify
The naturalness of this type of consciousness,
And point out to you that this is well within your human nature.

In fact, it is an intrinsic feature of being a non-physical consciousness *god perspective*,
Projecting as a physical imprint onto the physical world stage,
As a physical being on Earth:
Which You are, dear human being.

You see, you already have one foot in each world.
You are the unique non-physical-energy-frequency
That is a singular stream of the whole.

All the while, your intellect and body function
As marvellous tools that allow you to metabolise
Or transform non-physical energy into physical form.

Your intellect's ability to reason, plan, and visualise
Interprets this energy into ideas, intentions, and dreams.
At the same time, with its sensory and motor capabilities,
Your body acts as the implementer,
Converting these thoughts and intentions into action and expression in your world.

Your intellect and body serve as a wonderful conduit,
Transforming the invisible I AM or Divine energy
Into the visible manifestations of your lived experiences.

When you cook a meal, write an email, or laugh at a joke,
You are channeling your unique life force into these physical activities.
When you do any of these things, you will always do it differently from others.
Your expression in the physical world is unique.

Humans, by nature, are conduits of consciousness.
Human beings are channels.
If you were not, you would not exist.
You are vessels for a life-force energy
That flows through you, expressing itself outward
Into your physical reality.

## The Small Self Versus the I AM

Life force energy is another way of saying *I AM* energy,
Pointing to the most foundational, universal aspect of being:
That is God energy at the core of every living being,
Which connects you to the Universe, each other, and us.

This life force, or I AM energy,
Is as integral to your Being as your physical body,
With the whole (access to All-That-Is) within you.

At the same time, you know yourself as *You* on Earth:
This You that you are most familiar with,
Is a sectioned-off version of the whole,
Replete with ego and body,
That keeps you locked into your small self, or Earth identity.

Your small self with ego knows a consciousness
That is sectioned off so it can operate in your 3D physical world.
This sectioning off is what we have referred to
When we talk about an unintegrated psyche
Or parts of your consciousness that are not on show to you all the time –

Such as your memories, your subconscious mind, your dreams –
Much like a complex mosaic where each piece plays its role
In creating the bigger picture.
You could understand this also as different *states* of being.
This mosaic (your psyche) is partitioned,
Meaning that the full, holistic view of who you are
As a complete being is not always accessible to you in your daily lives.

This sectioning off allows you to identify
With the physicality of your world,
Form attachments to things, and develop
And operate from an ego-centric perspective,
Which is essential for your physical existence.
The ego provides you with a sense of individuality,
A sense of 'I' separate from the rest of the world:
To engage in oppositional experiences or be in a dyadic relationship with the external world.
To feel contrast, to have a choice, a preference,
And therefore, freedom to create.

However, it is really co-creation because your small self does not do this alone.

This may sound like a self-serving perspective,
Selfish or egotistical.
But this illusion of separateness is just to help preserve
Your physical body and experience for as long as possible.
It is a self-preservation mechanism that enables you to strive, survive, explore
And know the physical world from a unique perspective.

Your ego, too, is essential in understanding who you are.

However, the ego's perspective is necessarily limited.
It's like looking through a small window in a vast mansion.
It does not provide the full view of the entire mansion
(Which represents the entirety of our consciousness),
But rather, a small, focused perspective.

Your ego gives you a joyful experience
Of individuality in this physical world.
Yet it filters your experiences and perceptions through its narrow viewpoint,
While over-identification to your ego, and the conclusions it brings,
Can lead to much suffering.
And its limited perspective can sometimes cut you off
From a broader, more wholesome understanding
Of yourselves and greater perspectives of All-That-Is.

## Letting Divine Energy Flow for Creation and Fulfilment

However, you are a master harnesser of divine energy:
Able to receive, transduce, convert,
And direct inwardly and outwardly into your physical experience.

Marvel at what you have harnessed and channeled
In all humans have created on Earth
To make life more convenient and enjoyable!
You are adept at guiding and unifying disparate but innate forces within your world
To create practical (the wheel, the tool),
Powerful (electricity, wind power)
Or harmonious (music, art) things
That enrich your lived experience.

In orchestrating these energies, humans, like conductors,
Play a role in the magnificent symphony of life and innovation.
Therefore, let us demystify the word *channel*
And lighten its load,
Lessening any negative connotations you may have with it.

Remember that your ability to channel energy is inherently limitless,
Because consciousness is infinite and abundant.
It is a boundless resource that's always available,
Waiting to be tapped into and expressed in your physical world.

There is no end and no limit.

In fact, you already know this in the wholeness of who you are,
And this is why you chose to experience physicality in this way:

To create,
Explore,
Enjoy,
Expand,
Express,
Relate,
And love.

Thus, knowing it, beginning to really understand it,
And having it confirmed to you, live vibrantly!
Extract as much benefit, value, and enjoyment as you can from this knowledge!
Utilise, optimise, capitalise and maximise from this knowing:
Pursue moments of connection with the broader and higher aspects
Of your consciousness, the I AM that you are,
Thereby gaining a fuller, more holistic understanding
Of your true self and living the most enjoyable successful life,
However that looks to you.

# Expanding Into Love and Abundance

Many of you desire to channel higher states of consciousness,
And even create meaningful, enlightened engagement with other independent beings.
Raising your consciousness will allow you to open to such things
And gain higher wisdom and knowledge.
Doing so will not only positively impact your life,
But also the lives of others.

Most wonderfully, you channel the divine aspect of yourselves,
When you extend love and kindness to others,
Transcending the confines of the ego.

There is much fun and excitement to be had.
There is no end to what you can perceive, create, produce, and channel.
This includes material wealth, health, success and fulfilling relationships.

As we have said, we do not wish to prescribe how you must channel,
Or what you should expect to experience,
Because experience is unending and plentiful.

This is for you to co-create with All-That-Is.

CHAPTER

9

# Now is The Time.

## Joy in the Everyday Moments

Now is a good time,
Where you are most susceptible to knowing and really understanding.
Now we feel you are here to a place of hearing,
But also listening,
To begin the learning and teaching of this with which
You begin to know and feel is the truth and essence
Of your being-ness here in this physical world.

Those of you who are following,
Comprehending and feeling the resonation within yourselves, within your being,
Are in the perfect place to start to bring this awareness more and more
Into your everyday lives,
Allowing it to affect the ways of your being,
Operating and moving in the physical realm.

There is such joy to be had when you, the human,
Begin to cultivate and embed this awareness in your life,
This recognition of the marriage that is there;
The perfect union that exists within you
And the cultivation of the two parts of you
In coherence with each other.

Now, in this way, you can inform yourself of how things feel,
Intuit the path that is right for you,
Work with the array of phenomena and experiences that come your way,
And discern and choose according to vibration and non-physical cues,
Rather than ostensible appearances
And recollected mental imprinting.

It's not about a one-size-fits-all approach to life
But about finding your path.
By leading with vibration,
You can more effectively navigate your physical world.

It's about orienting by vibration first,
Then following up with action.
But the two go hand in hand.
The more you embody this, the more smoothly your journey unfolds,
Perfectly tailored to the unique energy flowing through You.

# The Perfect Union
# & Your Ascension Path

You see, a connection – to whom or what – does not really matter ultimately
If the vibration is high:
If the connection is of high frequency:
If the feeling and experience of consciousness feels good to you.

For whatever it may be,
It serves as a vehicle for knowing thyself and comprehending the oneness,
Unity and love of All-That-Is.
The form which appears to you is a unique interaction perfect for you as an agent for your growth.
Guiding you towards remembering the wholeness and perfection of your true nature.

Many may refer to this as an ascension path, and it is.
It is indeed a journey towards increasingly harmonious resonance with higher consciousness.
All beings possess this inherent greatness and wholeness to aspire to and identify with.
The more a being experiences this unity, the more blissful the feeling becomes.

Here we are, not just serving as an agent for Gayle
As she channels our energy data through her fingertips into the keyboard of her laptop,
But also as a guide for your spiritual journey.
As you read these words, they resonate with every aspect of your being,
Interacting with your entirety,
Even though you may not be aware of this as you read.

And so, on is the movement, upwards and forward.
This 'ascension path' is life's upward and forward momentum
As you experience it in physical form,
And even as we exist in our unique form of consciousness.
We exist within you, and you within us.
Everything is in everything, and we, along with you,
Are parts of a much greater whole.

No matter how splintered or separate you feel you may be,
Courtesy of your ego, you are still that:
A part of a much greater whole.
We hope that you can, at least in some aspect of your being, sense this union.

Here, Gayle is channeling,
And if you're grasping these words or feeling in alignment with them,
Then you are resonating with them in a non-physical sense,
Knowing on a *whole* level.
You may feel united by these words and notice a deep focus on the present moment.
You may feel at one with these words, and then notice how deeply you have become focused
On the *present*.

At this moment,
You may reconnect with the external world beyond these written words,
To the sensory experience of what is happening in the environment around you right now.
Here, we would like you to pause a moment
And appreciate the splendour of the two dimensions of *presence* unfolding before you:

Your internal feeling of non-physical resonance
And the marriage with the data stream that pours in from your physical environment
Through your physical senses.

Thus, you have the internal *and* external presence existing simultaneously, coherently.

We invite you to tap into this awareness as frequently as you are able.
This represents the integration of two worlds: the non-physical and the physical.
This marriage of two Selves,
This union of two realities,
This *whole* awareness can enrich your life on Earth in ways you may have never imagined.
It is a favourable marriage that will yield numerous benefits,
Leading to a fuller, more holistic understanding of who you are.

Here, we will pause and would like you to reflect on the practicalness and implementation of this Awareness.

All of this is said with love.

CHAPTER

10

# God and the Word

Here, we want to speak about the primal essence,
And how this may be understood by you.
While there are many references to this divine and profound understanding in your books,
*God* and the *Word*,
There is disagreement and controversy around why all that exists before you is here.

To know God is personal.
Therefore, a better understanding for you may come from your feeling and experience.
You also appreciate that it is intelligible and that knowing it
Is another side to understanding, that appeases your small self, mind and ego.

We encourage this feeling *and* reasoning
So you can gain a wholesome integration of who you are.
Rather than only existential abstraction or theoretical contemplation,
Although we understand that these paths, too, are possible ways to further understand this word of God.

# Discovering God Through Feelings and Experience

Then, what does the *Word* mean in relation to God?
The *Word* refers to the vibrational frequency
That reverberates through all of creation, resonating with the essence of God.
It is God in action.
All creation, everything that exists, stems from this original vibration or *Word*.

Manifesting visibly and invisibly.
Weaving the grand tapestry of creation and experience.
It exists beyond time.
Before, throughout, and after your current physical, earthly lifetime.

It is infinite, all-encompassing, and existing beyond and within you.
In this regard, the *Wor*d is the *action* of the essence of God
That seeks to know, experience, and love for the sake of learning itself.
You may think of its action as a distinct entity,
Yet unified and One.

It is *from* God and *is* God.
This provides the foundation for the divine relationship.
You, dear human, may be considered as both God and the Word.
For you are both *this* and also *that*.

What we mean with these words is that you are the essence of God
In a Universe where everything else carries this essence, too.
In you, there is a blending of individual and universal consciousness,
Where *this* represents your unique existence, and *that* represents the infinite expanse of God energy.

You are the vibrational frequency,
Embodying the harmony of God and manifesting physical existence.
You are the small self *and* I AM experiencing distinctness,
And yet simultaneously, you are *One* with God.
Understanding this concept expands consciousness,
Allowing you to realise your place within All-That-Is.

Thus, we would like you to acknowledge your divine identity,
And view your physical existence as a prism refracting this energy.
With your wonderful physical body and ego acting as the prism,
You are refracting or channeling divinity into all colours of human experience.

Each human being is a unique prism, creating a spectrum of expressions
That form individual lives while also being a holographic representation of the whole.
With the essence, the core, the macro and the micro reflection of all things simultaneously.
Mirroring vibration within All-That-Is by what you resonate with.
In relationship with yourself, each other and God.
All the while, you are an embodiment of love.

It may feel strange to refer to yourself as the *'I AM of God'*,
Unjustified or even unworthy,
But we assure you that you are absolutely worthy *and* justified,
Because this is the truth.

Therefore, declaring *I AM* is an acknowledgement and celebration of one's divine identity
And inherent worthiness.
And recognising *I AM that* appreciates the oneness
And equality in all beings and experiences.

Your small self ego-body and its attachments facilitate the flow of divine energy into your life.
They are temporary representations of You,
Acting as an *avatar* or *doer*:
Resonating, channeling, translating,
And anchoring the non-physical energy of God into the physical world.

You are the vibration of God.
You are the manifestation of God.
You are the experience of God.
You are the Word.
You are *of* God and *with* God.

Therefore, look into every face that you see and recognise God, too.
When you bring into your awareness all other beings you know or may not know,
You are knowing them too to be God,
And we hope you begin to remember this while you interact with others.

That this is the love story or relationship of God with and unto itself.
The experience and reach of God is infinite, refracting infinitesimally.
While the whole is contained within the stream or fractal, it remains perfect,
No matter how large or small.
It is everything, every now, every place, every experience, everyone.

Each thought, word, and action channels the divinity of the *Word*,
Shaping reality and contributing to the cosmic perfection of All-That-Is.
Embracing this understanding will enable you to live a harmonious, expansive, and joyous experience on Earth.
You are indescribable perfection.
You are the many names and pathways of God.
You are the way, the truth and the light.

CHAPTER

11

# Love and the Action of Love

In a state of love, we find the essence of divine understanding,
And in this, the core of your *being* is revealed.
Feeling and acting from love is the simplest form of knowing
The I AM-ness of who you are.
By feeling love, we refer to it in all its active and passive forms.

Active love is expressed through conscious expressions
Like acts of kindness, empathy, compassion, understanding, and service.
It visibly influences the world with higher frequency consciousness.

Passive love resides quietly within,
Representing feelings of peace, well-being, contentment, joy, and unity.
Even in silence, reflecting the underlying love that is always present.

Love is not just an emotion,
But a vibrational frequency that permeates the entirety of existence.
It is the fundamental building block of All-That-Is.
It is God's energy underpinning all of creation,
And manifesting as matter,
It informs the laws of physics.

When the intention behind your thoughts, behaviours and actions
Is of a feeling of union, love, wholeness, integration
And the feeling of wanting to be well or do well,
It enables you to recognise the face of God in another also:
To recognise that you are a unique viewpoint of God
Interplaying and sharing experience with another being.

This recognition is like creating an energetic loop that feeds back to you,
Culminating in a greater sense of joy for your life.
Your feelings of love heighten awareness,
Are life-affirming and strengthening your connection to the I AM Self
And All-That-Is.

To give and receive love is to take full advantage of the unique physical perspective you are in,
For it allows you to experience non-physical energy as a distinct person:
Giving and receiving to *another* uniquely focused being.
For you, dear human, these are tangible experiences of divine energy,
And they nourish both aspects of yourself and the world around you.

Feeling love also means allowing yourself to receive it,
Reaffirming that you are an energy being,
And able to receive and be aware of this non-physical energy
Because you *feel* it.
Loving energy can be shared and passed between all beings.
Awareness of this raises consciousness.

The experience of giving and receiving love transcends the physical.
Yet it nourishes both you and the other party, as the action carries the essence of the union –
Of that which you both are.
This is the reason why it feels so good.
Because it affirms the truth of union between all things.

Therefore, anything you do in your life that is of this intention
Will affirm and strengthen your connection to All-That-Is.
Love is both the expression and the vehicle of divine energy.
Forming the fabric of God's being and the lens through which God experiences itself.
It is the core principle guiding the evolution of consciousness.
It serves as a reminder of interconnectedness and shared origin in All-That-Is.

Every being is both a product of love and a vessel for its expression.
The capacity to love and form meaningful connections manifests the divine principle at work,
Propelling beings toward unity, understanding, and co-creation.
Look upon your world and everything in it with unconditional *eyes* of love,
And see God in everything.
When you truly begin to see this, your life will ascend to new heights of freedom and joy.

## Loving Action

What is loving action?
Keeping awareness of it can transform your daily life experience.
It involves approaching all your actions with an intention rooted in love,
Fostering a deeper connection to the present moment and everything you do.

All actions, even the most mundane,
Can be carried out with an underlying intention of love.
It is truly an embodiment of the I AM and divinity in form.

Loving action does not just refer to overt gestures or displays of affection,
But rather a fundamental attitude that permeates
Every decision made, every word spoken, and every activity undertaken.
We understand that this may be difficult to practise all the time
As you move around in your physical world with your egos running on auto-pilot.

Before you start any task,
Take a moment to connect with your Higher, I AM Self.
Reflect upon your interconnectedness with all that exists,
And tap into the feeling of gratitude for your physical experience.
The feelings of connection and gratitude embody the essence of love,
And incorporating them into your actions can transform any task into a Loving Action.

Gratitude is your connection to All-That-Is, to the I AM,
And to the Oneness of all existence.
Gratitude is a mirroring back of God's energy.
By cultivating feelings of love, connection, and gratitude,
You can elevate your vibrational frequency,
Aligning yourself with experiences and interactions that resonate more profoundly
With your true essence.
Although this energy is non-physical,
It influences your experiences in the physical world.

## Your Wide-Ranging Circle of Love

Remember to extend this feeling of connection, not just to people,
But also to the natural world.
Connect with loving intention to the plants, trees, earth, sky, water,
And the diverse array of animals that share your planet.

By establishing this connection and by channeling loving action,
You are reinforcing the feedback loop of love,
And the understanding that you are the holographic human,
Containing the essence of God and All-That-Is.
Through Loving Action, you can create a more meaningful, fulfilling, and joyous life.

Loving action extends beyond physical acts
And encompasses intentions, thoughts, and emotional responses as well.
It is important to remember that these, shown in response to others,
reflect the love you hold for yourself.

The care, respect, and compassion you extend to others are mirrored back to you,
Affirming your inherent worth and divine nature.
We have spoken about the fact that loving, respecting and caring for yourself,
Is an excellent place to begin to acknowledge and implement in your life
The working knowledge of you as God-Self in physical form.

However, we understand that some of you will find it easier
To demonstrate this to another being in a way that offers your visual data as feedback
Before you develop the confidence to deliberately practise this loving action towards yourself.

We would like you to know, however, that there is no loving action that you can do
That does not vibrate into yourself that does not end within your being.
For the transmission of loving intention and loving action comes from you
And will surely and definitely be received back from the largest mirror of All-That-Is to you.

## The Impact of Loving Action

Every act of loving kindness, regardless of its size or the visibility of its impact,
Contributes to the collective vibrational frequency.
Loving action towards others doesn't have to be big and sweeping.
It can also be in the small kindnesses.
The action does not need you to stay for the results.
The intention and the vibration are merely enough.

However, we know you will feel satisfaction
If you are sometimes able to see the effects of your loving actions.
Remember you are in a vibration-oriented experience,
So the intention and vibration behind your actions are far more significant
Than the immediate, observable results.

You don't have to witness the fruits of your kindness
To know that it has had an impact.
You may simply wish someone well without verbally expressing it,
And this will be an act of love.

Your intentions, positive thoughts, and silent blessings send out vibrations
That touch others in ways you may not see.
This is the law of vibration.

Your vibration is what is transmitted,
And though you may not see physical signs that this is so,
Know that this is law.

Vibration raises your frequency and connects you more strongly to love and to All-That-Is.
This does not mean, either, that you are doing this merely to look after yourself
And your own Connection.
It is done simply for the joy of love.

Engaging in Loving Action raises your vibrational frequency,
Connecting you more closely with All-That-You-Are.

We remind you that your physical experience begins in the non-physical realm,
A divine, miraculous imaginal realm communicated to you through your imagination.
Thus, your imagination can help you shape your intentions and loving actions in your world,
Focusing your energy on higher ways of being.

CHAPTER 12

# Love is the Basis of Everything

Now you understand that loving action is the connection, gratitude,
And intention towards something.
We would like you to reflect on those things or people in your life
That do not give you comfort and do not make you feel happy.

Consider every experience you have in your physical life,
Even those that cause discomfort, unhappiness and an array of negative feelings for you.
We would like you to understand that all experience is ultimately rooted in love.
Unwanted experiences, too, are prompts for your growth,
Shaping your personality and driving your evolution.
They create a contrast that helps to better understand what you prefer and what you don't,
Thus shaping your unique path.
The intention behind these things is to offer you a perspective that precipitates vibration in you,
Gives you something to dislike,
And that disliking shapes and propels you more and more towards your progression.

Even though these elements elicit negative emotions,
They are the agents for your illumination, exploration, and later joy.
They intend to provide direction or perspective,
Prompting a response taking you to ever-new experiences.

These things give you multiple attraction points, vibrationally speaking.
Hence, you continue to pull into your life a constant mixture of experiences.
Ranging in emotion from better to worse, worse to better and so on,
So that you can pivot yourself and your vibration.
Hone and sculpt yourself and your way of living.
Yours is a time-bound journey that leads you to experience new consciousness.
Consider this a grand exploration into the physical realm of Earth,
Where you are keen to experience self versus *other*.
This dyadic pattern of contrasts.

So all things, good and bad, positive and negative,
Are there, lovingly (with loving intention) for your experience in the physical world
For your growth, learning and ascension path.
The path where you can realise in greater and greater increments
Your Union with All-That-Is.

Therefore, do not fear when things seem bleak or down.
Know that there is great wisdom
To all of the things you come across during your physical experience,
And charging your life with loving action will yoke into your being the power of the I AM.

It will also yoke in the feeling of connection.
Even in times of difficulty, remember this connection.
Know that you are always guided, loved, and supported by your divine 'I AM' essence.
Each experience is an invitation to deepen your understanding of love and who you truly are.
Each adversity you may encounter is a gift:
A divine hand of spiritual direction.

All within the divine plan.
All is well.
Therefore, we say again, do not fear when things seem difficult.
Know that there is wisdom in every experience you encounter.

When faced with individuals who are entangled in negativity,
Remember their journey is likely challenging.
They might not see a way out of their lower vibrational patterns
That are consequently attracting similar experiences.

There might be fear holding them back,
And they may feel as if they are adrift at sea.
Despite their actions, remember they too are expressions of the divine,
Just experiencing life through a different lens.
If you can't help them directly, wish them well as they navigate their unique path to enlightenment.
Recognise that their presence in your life can catalyse your growth, too.

Therefore, practising gratitude acknowledges the pervasive love that connects all beings,
Regardless of their awareness of it.
Remember, beneath it all is Love, Union, and God.

CHAPTER 13

# Wonder

Wonder in this world is a beautiful thing.
By wonder we mean the interest, fascination and joy of what you see before you.

This feeling is a heightened vibrational experience,
And we encourage you to seek out and revel in moments that bring wonder to you.

Wonder is the divine within you,
Marvelling at the creation you encounter during your physical experience.

In children, this feeling comes easy,
For they are more connected with their I AM Self,
And they are more present.

Therefore, we encourage you to approach your physical world with child-like wonder,
In awe of the experience and phenomena that come before you.
As it has manifested from All-That-Is
And is a reflection of you and your vibrational output.

Much of what you will encounter in your world is a shared vibrational rendering.
By that, we mean that you agree on the existence and functioning of certain things.

However, they are a marvel, nonetheless.
Taking time to acknowledge all of this gives you another opportunity to connect to the I AM self,
To love and All-That-Is.

Growing awareness of your feelings and emotions and how they change
Allows you to sense the vibration accompanying each emotion.
It is a step towards anchoring awareness of the non-physical aspect of you in daily life.

Soon, we feel you will be marvelling in wonder more
At the vibration you feel within your physical body!
This can lead to witnessing better and quicker manifestations in your life.
This evolutionary path will become synchronistic with vibration and resonance
And experiences beyond the physical realm,
Transcending the need for a physical body.
In real terms, you would see the lag between space and time in your 3D world lessen
As you learn to manifest your wishes synergistically, synchronistically,
And, therefore, more instantaneously.

Wonder is another bridge for you,
Between your physical ego-body life and the non-physical energy being that you are.
Use this bridge to cultivate your sense of God-Self,
And anchor this awareness into your everyday moments.

# The Architecture of Self

## From the Cosmos You Emerge

## Who Are you?

Let's delve into the roots of your being,
Exploring who you are, what you embody, how you merge with all of creation.

You, in your daily existence, resonate most with your human identity,
Your physical and mental self,
A complex interaction of body and mind, defining your unique identity.

This is your physical appearance, your name, personality,
And the facts that you associate with yourself,
Such as your ethnic origin, the place you live, the way you spend your time,
The relationships you have with people,
And how you come to be known in and around your surroundings.

## You Are Infinite, Metaphysical Consciousness

Your concept of Self is formed from a plethora of labels
Based on your preferences, values, behaviours and beliefs.
However, as we have explained, and as you may be aware,
There is a *You* behind You:
A You beyond, within and around all of this
That is infinite, knowing, loving and has pre- and post-existed your current physical form
Before your imagined time you came into this physical world.

We say *imagined* because time is only real for your existence
While experiencing the physical body.
Therefore, it may be better to say that there is a *You*
That envelops your time here, now, in this physical body.

This is the consciousness that observes your thinking
And follows your mood that is present always,
Even while you experience different states of being,
Such as sleeping and dreaming.
It is the aspect that even observes your conscious withdrawal from the physical body
When you fully reemerge into the non-physical realm.
It is the transmission of I AM energy through your physical body.
At the same time, it interacts with the program of ego identity
Throughout your earth life.

# Ego As a Temporary Programme

We say *programme,* because it is temporary,
And implemented by the larger, non-physical aspect of Who-You-Are.
It is an instrument for you to mediate and perceive in the physical world.

This programme gets written and imprinted with your experiences,
Values, beliefs, habits, behaviours and memories.
This programme is the *you* you identify with most of the time,
But is only helpful for your physical world.

In this respect, your Self can be experienced from two perspectives:
The smaller ego self and the larger I AM Self.

## A Two-Perspective Vantage Point

The small ego self is a projection of the non-physical I AM Self into the physical plane,
Constrained by space and time constraints.
Conversely, the I AM Self exists outside these boundaries,
And is present, infinite and multidimensional.
You may know it as your Higher Self or your non-physical Self.

We use multiple ways of describing to give you various pathways into understanding.
Still, essentially, we are referring to something that is one and the same.

Your I AM Self or Higher Self, is embodied in a unique energy frequency.
This particular frequency, though individual in its expression,
Emanates from a universal, all-encompassing source,
Which extends infinitely to countless other unique expressions.
The origin of this energy is an omnipresent stream of God energy
That infuses every aspect of creation.
Therefore, you and all things in existence are intricately linked through this union.
Because you emanate from the same source.

Consider your sun the boundless sphere of radiating light,
Shining upon everything on Earth.
This omnipotent sun symbolises God, or All-That-Is,
An infinite, multidimensional essence beyond the confines of space and time.
The sun is ever-present, shedding its light universally,
Representing God and its energy.

Next, we would like you to envision specific places on Earth
Where the sun's light uniquely shines,
Illuminating each with particular intensity and angle,
Subject to the cycles of day and night and the changing seasons,
Creating contrast and shadows.
These individual rays of light symbolise the I AM Self.

The places where the rays fall and cast shadows signify the smaller ego selves:
The shadows are the manifested human.
Localised projections bound by the physical realities of space and time.
Each shadow experiences the sun's light differently,
Bounded by its geography, climate, and temporal patterns,
Akin to your individual earthly existences with their limitations and unique experiences.

Remarkably, each place that the sun illuminates
Carries a unique expression of the sun's vast energy –
Like your ego selves embodying the projection of the non-physical I AM Self.
Each stream of light projection, no matter where it is, is connected to the sun,
Embodying its warmth and light in ways that align with their unique earthly conditions.
The shadow, however, is an after-projection,
And will form and disappear over and over again.
It is a temporary co-creation with the physical world.
Yet the sun's rays are constant.

In the dance of light and shadow, the smaller ego self – the individual shadow –
Exists as a focused expression of the larger God Self – the sun.
While each place (shadow) experiences moments of brightness and darkness,
The sun, the source of their illumination, remains constant, infinite, and unbounded.
This is the beginning of understanding the architecture of the Self.

All energy and its streams, all forms of consciousness,
Exist simultaneously and are holographic in principle.
This means that even though your current physical experience may feel separated and distinct,
You carry within you the entirety of the divine source energy –
Reflecting the divinity of All-That-Is.

## The Significance of Now

We want to add to all of this:
Transmission, refraction, projection, manifestation and experiencing the energy of God
Transpires in the 'Now.'

This concept is significant,
Especially in understanding your higher I AM Self.

There is only a present moment in All-That-Is,
Which may be hard for you to conceptualise,
But time with a past and future are just relative to your earthly realm of physical being,
And are there to help you move progressively through your environment,
In what (to you) seems like a sequence of action.

In your physical existence, your ego self perceives time linearly
As past, present, and future.
It is different from this in the non-physical of All-That-Is.
However, to say that there is only one moment in time is also slightly misleading,
Although we offer this to help comprehension:

There is no time,
Therefore no categorisation of past, present or future.

Ponder an All-That-Is without getting into details in your mind:
An *'Is-ness'* of Being.

All beginnings and endings without end or beginning;
Whole, complete, perfect.
All at once.
*Still* in its essence.

A confluence of so many streamed entities of vibration,
Like *instruments* of frequency,
All profoundly resonating in infinite directions and degrees,
That paradoxically creates an overall truth of love, stillness and perfection.
We know this may be hard to understand because you exist within it,
Deeply embedded in the physical realm.
With your focus pointed (much of the time)
Through your eyes, ears, nose and mouth;
Engaged in the external reality of your earth environment.

To understand how this might be so,
Let us reflect on what you know about light:

In a spectrum, each colour represents a different frequency of light waves.
Usually, these colours are distinct and occupy a specific place in the spectrum.
However, when all these diverse frequencies come together at an extremely high speed,
They converge into one singular manifestation of white light, representing pure, unified energy.
This is how so many frequencies of being and consciousness in all of creation,
Merge on the most expanded scale into pure bright light, stillness and perfection.

If you relate this analogy to the existence of All-That-Is,
And the idea of the eternal now that we describe,
Every vibrational transmission of energy is like a colour in the spectrum of reality.
These colours are continuously occurring, interacting, and interweaving
In the ever-present *Now*.

Despite appearing distinct in your earthly perception and creating a myriad of manifestations,
They are, in essence, part of a singular, omnipresent reality.

As vibration and consciousness become higher, the veils of distinction dissolve.
Separation vanishes, and a unified field of pure, perfect, undivided existence remains –
Similar to how separate colours fuse into a coherent, white light in the realm of optics.

However, it is possible for you to understand this through non-physical experience.
But it is more challenging to understand this through the intellect,
Because it goes against the very parameters that your ego identifies with in this physical world.

For you, it is more the case of believing or *feeling*,
Despite what you see around you.
Everything exists all at once, holographically.
Although everything in creation is constantly in flux and vibration,
This continuous change is a unified field
That sustains integrity and unchanging truth at its core.

This paradoxical combination of dynamic motion and unalterable stillness
Encapsulates the timeless nature of divine energy,
Manifesting as the ongoing, eternal *Now*.

We know this can be challenging to relate to daily
As you move around the places you inhabit and pass the time in your world.
You see your world full of binary qualities that provide contrast and polarity,
Creating a convincing illusion of matter, boundaries and limits.

However, beyond this paradox,
Beyond these binary qualities,
There is a Oneness, a Union.
You ultimately contain everything within you.

*You are the sun's ray.*

# Reverence For Your Higher Self

Your Higher Self is the streamlined, unique, non-physical I AM energy
That is beaming within and around you.
A signature frequency containing a desire for physical experience in this moment.
It is the part of you connected to divine wisdom and guidance,
Mediating between your human experience and All-That-Is.

This Higher Self desires to experience certain lessons during its time in a physical form.
It is the blueprint of personality, yet resonates with All-That-Is.

The Higher Self is your spiritual essence,
Transcending the physical death,
Considered the true Self or identity,
Connected to the source or God.

All of you receive non-physical communication from your Higher Self.
You will know it as:
Intuition, feeling, inspiration, dreams, ambitions, desires, curiosity, excitement and wonder.
You will also feel it through loving action.
You will feel its communication by how good you feel about something.
This is the vibrational feeling of alignment, that we have spoken about.

We reiterate that this vibrational feeling of alignment or misalignment
Is carried through your range of emotional experiences,
Where you feel better or worse, according to how in alignment you are resonating
With your Higher Self.

We desire you to listen more closely to this feeling,
Because it is your lifeline or life energy.
It is surely the best guide that truly harmonises your life path
And sense of love and Self-hood.

## Synergy in an Even More Expansive Sense of Self

However, this Higher Self comes forth from and is nested within
An even more expansive sense of Self, a *group Self,* so to speak,
Which some may refer to as an *oversoul*.

The Group self is a broader sense of Self,
A larger, collective, spiritual reality and a more expansive energy perspective
With a shared purpose of evolution.
It has an over-arching desire to experience *themes*.

We say *themes,* because the lessons and desires for experience are broader
Than those of the Higher Self.
The group Self resonates within and is organised from
An even more expansive consciousness of All-That-Is.
It has a collective consciousness,
Yet it generates directives for individual experience:
Multiple lives, which you will understand as happening in different locations and time-frames,
But are simultaneous.
As everything happens in the *now*.

The group self, too, is a source of wisdom and illumination for you
Because you are part of it.
You are nested within the Higher Self,
Which is nested within the group self.
Some of you will be able to intuit or channel consciousness from this broader perspective,
Or from the other manifestations of life experience it generates.
All of this remains God-energy that is focused from the broad to the narrow,
From the macroscopic down to the microscopic forms of consciousness.

However, as we have said, everything is holographic,
So even within the smallest fractals of god energy,
You can tap into the energy and union of the whole.

The Group Self wishes to accumulate experience in groups or sets.
Streaming into multiple perspectives simultaneously and synergistically.
By *synergistically,* we mean the cooperative action of separate but interconnected perspectives,
Where the overall collective experience is equally cherished.

Each perspective within the Group Self
Brings a unique viewpoint and experience to the collective,
Creating a multidimensional and more comprehensive understanding of existence
Than any single perspective could offer.

So, by experiencing multiple perspectives simultaneously and synergistically,
The Group Self is exploring and experiencing group consciousness.
This is energy projection that is multi-tasking –
Feeling, exploring, accumulating, embodying the experience for the sake of experiencing itself,
Expanding multiple Beings synergistically, coherently and lovingly.
This is an organising faction of God-ness and All-That-Is
That is part of the cyclical nature of all creation.

There is a division and a coming together in perfect harmony.
For we would like to remind you of the Oneness of all and the perfection of it all.
Therefore, you may be aware that you are part of something much greater and bigger
And are included fully in this greatness.
You are part of this.
You are identifying as a unique energy stream in physical form
That is here to play and enjoy, learn and grow, pivot, expand and move forward
Through your time-space experience, sequentially,
Revelling in the physicality and all aspects of polarity that come with it.
You are an individual.
Yet you can channel aspects of this group consciousness into your life.
You are a Higher Self,
And you are a Group Self, too.

## You Are the Perfect Amalgamation

You are the amalgamation of spiritual, mental, and physical aspects.
The more you acknowledge and remain aware in daily life,
The more connectivity, perception, inspiration and creativity you will feel
And the more enabled you will be to actualise your divine potential.

Some of you may glimpse or experience fragments of greater connection
Or vibrational resonance with these other Self-streams within your group self.
You may interpret them as past lives.
However, there is no past in the non-physical,
Only nowness, with which you are resonating.

It does not matter if you feel no awareness or resonance with other forms of Self.
What matters more is you feel the greater connection to All-That-Is:
To the I AM that you are.

## You Are Nested Layers

Beyond the Group Self,
There are higher vibrational organisations of God consciousness
That oversee the arrangement and focus of energy and experience.
There is a rhythm, a vibration, a cyclical, causal impulse of creation and regeneration
In an infinite array of well-ordered and purposeful experiences,
Where love and knowing itself are the divine plan.

Beyond the Group Self exists a higher and broader consciousness.
Akin to a cluster or collection of groups selves, or oversouls.
Formed from a directive to experience a more general theme
In a particular realm or dimension.
For ease, you can refer to this as a master group.
You may also think of this as *being* on a *meta* level.
But this does not mean it is superior.
It represents a higher level of unity and resonance.
You can think of it as an engine, a perpetuator, a creative essence of issuing forth impulses,
Directives, ambitions and causal frequencies.
It subtly guides the flow of divine energy,
Organising and influencing the patterns of existence.

The consciousness of the master group has less definition.
By this, we mean there is less form to articulate.
Yet there is still form, as non-physical energy.
Master groups channel God energy,
Focusing specific levels of consciousness towards various realms and dimensions,
Where group selves are contained, composing unique experience themes.
Master groups can be likened to large prisms,
Refracting into group selves.
By *prisms,* we mean master groups refract God's light of consciousness
Into perspectives or dimensions of influence over group selves.
They are a higher directive of diversity or energy into various forms or experiences.

The Higher Self is nested within the group self
Which is nested within the master group.
These clusters of directed master group energy are generated by the highest energy of All-That-Is, *God*, to experience itself.

Let's call it the *original impulse*.
This is the force that sets everything in motion.
It is less formed, less causal and more impulsive.
By this, we mean it acts more spontaneously and freely.
It is an initiating, creative force without being structured.

The original impulse is All-That-Is consciousness:
The active force of God energy,
Pervasive and setting all of creation in motion.
It is love in action,
And the vehicle for God to experience itself.

This divine energy spreads through all creation,
Producing vibrational relationships, resonances or organisations.
It comes from a single point of union or source,
Which is God:

We say *point,* but it is different from how you know it.
We mean that it is *One, non-dual, whole, perfect, pure, absolute*:
So still and light that you may think of it as disappearing into itself.
It is a universal intelligence that encompasses everything.
Yet it gives birth to the manifold expression of itself.

All of these layers which we speak of *are* God and are nested within.
Thus, all is contained within the All.

There is a progression of consciousness
From the most non-dual Oneness
To the infinite fragments and streams of manifested physical form – the human body.

Therefore, within God is a gradation of frequencies,
Including its unified Self and all of its streamed fractalised experiences.

# God Into Self: A Metaphor

Divine One, we would again like to use the metaphor of your sun:

Imagine God as the *space* that holds the sun.
The space represents the source of all energy, consciousness and light.
It is the Oneness and origin that makes everything else possible.
Now imagine God's Energy or the *original impulse*, as the sun itself.
This is the primal energy and instinct to experience itself in motion.
It is the divine emanator of light, love and consciousness.
It is also the original active power and energy.
The energy is undefined and unstructured,
But resonating from the sun's core,
That sets everything into motion.

Then, we ask you to consider the enormous solar flares of the sun
That burst forward with initiatives of direction and energy.
They are powerful organisers,
Just like the master groups directing the energy and helping to shape how it is used.
With this aspect of the solar flares, like the *master groups*,
There is a more defined focus directed into particular realms.

Now, consider the group self as springing from the master group.
This is akin to focused beams of sun energy that come from the solar flares.
These beams are smaller and more focused than the larger solar flares,
And have a specific direction and purpose,
Concentrating the sun's energy in particular locations and levels of manifestation.

Then consider the Higher Self, springing from the group self.
The individual rays created from the strong beams of the sun represent the Higher Selves,
Focused into progression from the group self.
Imagine these as the individualised, singular rays of sunlight reaching Earth.
They are individual expressions of the sun's energy,
Each unique, yet non-physical.
Just as you are individual streams of Higher Self.
This is how the energy that is God manifests into you.
This is the I AM of who you are.
The divine god energy shining *as you* and through you.

Lastly, consider the individualised, separated ray of the sun cast into the physical realm.
It interacts with its physical environment,
And it appears as a shadow.
It is made from contrast;
It is now in the physical realm,
Yet, it depends on its physical and non-physical parts to be recognised as it is.
This is you, the human being.
Made from the stream of light and consciousness that is your Higher Self,
Fused with the physical realm.
Like the spots on Earth where the sunlight touches,
Where the rays create warmth and light,
And where life can flourish because of the sun's energy.
This is you, able to thrive and interact,
Creating an experience that is entirely unique to you.

While we provide a metaphor to inspire your understanding of the way you are part of everything
And the path you have, which is divine,
We appreciate that language gives consciousness a narrower form.

Even by attempting to describe the indescribable,
The human mind will grasp what it can,
Yet it caps its understanding with the limitations of language.
This is why it is better sometimes to encourage your awareness beyond the faculties of the mind.

Here, imagination can take over from language.

## A Unity Consciousness

Earnestly seek an embodiment of this awareness in your daily life
By living with loving action and acknowledgement
Without inhibiting the channeling of I AM energy into your present moment
To experience what you may consider *ineffable*.
By doing this, you will feel more connected,
Than by trying to give the formless form with the use of language.

However, we would like to impart this:
Although there are limitations and restrictions
In physical processing and comprehension of Gayle's physical form,
Because she is intrinsically encased and bound by physical dimensionality,
She knows, and you know, at your deepest core of being,
What is there, what it is we describe,
And the nature of All-That-Is.
For you have it folded within you, holographically.
You are within it, and the whole is within you.
You may be a focused stream or streamlined version of God-Self,
But you are not a slice off from, or cut off, from the whole.

However minuscule the streamlining of energy,
However, often the energy of the whole is divided,
It remains whole, perfect, complete
With the Oneness and union still intact.

We would like to finish this part of describing the architecture of the Self
By saying that ultimately and finally, all of this,
Beyond the subtle, causal and impulsive realm of All-That-Is,
Is the stillness, perfection and pure, deep love of God.

Imagine a broader consciousness with invisible hands
That steer the manifestation of cosmic coherence:
Movement and stillness,
Lightness and darkness,
Divisionary and unifying,
Visible and invisible,
Empty and full, all at once.
An amazingly complex, multifaceted reality,
Yet remarkably simple.

Your human mind is considered the perfect arena
Where the Self's physical and non-physical aspects can meet and achieve
Integration and unity of consciousness.
You are here to achieve the marriage of these two aspects.
You cannot go wrong, because you are already here.
We simply remind your consciousness of it.

CHAPTER

15

# Time and Space

We would like you to understand an aspect of time and space
So that you have context in relation to feeling the connection to yourself and All-That-Is.
This will also be helpful to your understanding of contact with other beings,
For there are other realms that either do not have the parameters of time and space,
Or who experience time in a different way than you do on Earth.

# The Illusion of Time and Space

Time is part of the fabric of All-That-Is.
It is an aspect of reality in material and evolutionary worlds like yours.
It is tied to your perception of having events appear sequentially.
In this way, you can see the relationship between cause and effect,
And you can expect things to happen linearly,
Which gives an impression of progression in your life.

In the present, your ideas of past and future,
Imaginings and memories have a platform,
For there is no other platform for them to be housed.
Because there is no past or future.
Thus, the present moment of *Now* is eternal.

## The Eternal Now

*Now* is where you feel a connection to the I AM,
To higher consciousness and being-ness,
With all facets of consciousness and experience you can resonate with.

For example, in the present now, you can feel and hear your breath.
However, as soon as you engage with your memories,
You have disengaged with the presence of your breath.
As soon as you begin to worry about the future,
You have disengaged with the presence of your breath.

Also, in the here and now,
You can engage with your feelings,
Access your internal vibration indicator,
And acknowledge how in *alignment* you are with the I AM self.
You can feel what you are transmitting energetically, too.

# Unify With the Here and Now

If you feel good, you are in alignment with the I AM energy that flows through you.
If you feel bad, you are out of alignment with the I AM energy.
When you are feeling bad, there is a sense of *separation*
From your natural state of being.

That sense of separation feels as though you have disconnected
From the natural happy place where you should be.
The feeling alone is enough to make you understand that it is not as pleasant as it could be,
And you are not as happy as you could be.
This is your personal indicator that you are off-track,
Or need to reconnect with your higher life-force energy of All-That-Is.

Bad feelings are not meant to be tolerated for their own sake.
They are there to make you uncomfortable enough to look for relief and ease!
They are there to pronounce contrast in your experience,
So you can choose, based on what feels right for you.
Your emotions are clear indicators of this.

By raising this point,
We illustrate that knowing this,
You may understand the idea that there is only one time for All-That-Is.
Because the real indicator of how you are feeling
Can be found in the present moment.
There is no time in truth,
And no time in the non-physical realm,
Just vibration and your *consciousness* or *awareness* of it.
An *Is-ness* or Being-ness that is infinite, eternal, absolute, Divine.

However, you, in your human perspective,
Have time and space to serve your physical experience,
To move through and interact with your environment.
You are embodied in a world of denser energy,
Where things appear solid and tangible,
So you can experience vibration as *things* interactively,
Such as places, objects, and events.
This is to give the representation of sequential experience:
Moving through time and, therefore, space, progressively.
It allows you to learn from the past, live in the present, and plan for the future.
Moreover, your awareness of time fuels the pursuit of progress
As you strive to grow, change, and evolve.

Time and space are tied together and work well with your ego self,
Enabling joy in being active,
Joy in the beginnings and endings,
And enjoyment in what is the time *in between*.
When your awareness is on these *in between* moments,
Time becomes sacred.
Because it is acknowledgement of the now.

Therefore, your presence in the now,
As often as you can bring your consciousness to it,
Allows you to experience this universal truth, however you can.
Experiencing a deep presence in the now will feel good because it is true.
It is you in alignment with it.

# Embracing the Timeless Actuality

You may only fully grasp this timeless actuality once you evolve spiritually
And gain expanded consciousness.
It is what we encourage you towards.

Meanwhile, enjoy this time-space physical experience.
Remember that this is a stepping stone towards your eventual realisation
Of All-That-Is.

During this physical experience,
You will witness nothing permanent throughout your life journey.
The only permanent thing is what you are aware of
When you connect with the I AM and its aspects.
You will see that human life appears to have a definitive beginning and end,
Marked by birth and death.

However, what you perceive as *death* is merely a transition,
A change in density rather than an absolute end.

Though the physical body may cease to function,
Your I AM energy stream continues its experience and consciousness,
Carrying your unique personality and cultivated character,
The individual energy stream of God energy that you are.

This non-physical I AM You,
Unbounded by physical limitations,
Continues its existence in higher consciousness.

Therefore, while the physical body has a beginning and end,
The I AM Self is eternal,
Transcending the temporal experiences of biological life.

Whether you remember it or not,
You are part of All-That-Is,
In physical form,
Perfect, whole and always holographic.

Time and space are vital for your unfolding physical life and spiritual potential.
Consider this physical experience as a moving image of eternity,
A living tableau, constantly updating and reconfiguring,
Upon which the experience of existence plays out.
To you, it appears as if you age through time and experience across a lifespan.

Your journey is not just a passage through checkpoints of ageing and experience,
But an ongoing synchronisation
With the ever-unfolding quantum aspect of consciousness.
In reality, every aspect of potentiality and possibility is already laid out!

Where every possibility, every potential moment, already coexists in an eternal *now*.
Within which every conceivable experience is like a coordinate,
Permanently possible, yet dynamically interconnected.

Your conscious awareness navigates through the sequential moments of experiences,
Creating the illusion of a flowing timeline.
However, it is more like a boundless landscape of moments in a unified field.
Therefore, every moment of *now* you experience
Is a gateway into infinite possibilities and pathways.
This is why, in every moment, you can tap into how you feel,
And your feelings shall indicate to you,
Like a pathway lighting up,
The possibilities that are most in alignment with you.

The more conscious you are of this,
The more you practise this awareness daily,
And the more grounded you will become in the non-linear, non-physical reality
Beyond your physical life.
You will find more incredible synchronicity, more ease and flow.
You may notice that your desires materialise more quickly and more easily.

The more you notice this,
The more you'll understand that manifestation happens via your vibrational transmission:
The greater the connection you will feel to higher consciousness,
And therefore, a more conscious connection and perspective on the events in your life,
Your relationships and connection to other human beings:
To animal, plant and mineral consciousness on your Earth,
And to other realms and dimensions of being too.

You will become less fearful of physical death
Because your connection to the infinite and greater sense of Who-You-Are
Will surpass the scope of the limited, temporal, finite understanding of your physical experience.
The more you let go of the fear of death,
The more you'll truly live!

Yes, indeed, you will lose your fear of dying.
Because there is no such thing as *death* to the greater eternal stream of who you are.

CHAPTER

# 16

# Channeling (Part 2)

## The Potentiality of Vibration

Now we have explained the pervasive consciousness,
Infinity, eternity, love and divinity that is God, All-That-Is.
Now, we have explained that time and space are helpful constructs
To assist in your physical experience
And that Being in the present moment,
Participating in loving action and wonder are aligning aspects for you,
We would like to remind you to reconnect
With another true constant of measurement
To bridge your non-physical Self with your physical Self:
Vibration.
Your internal vibration indicator is your tool to connect
With any facet of creation and frequency within it.

Your internal vibration indicator,
The way you understand if something feels good to you,
Whether you are in resonance with it,
Enables you to connect with any facet of creation you desire.
It allows you to integrate with your non-physical, Higher Self. The I AM.
This alignment connects you with a greater field of consciousness,
And higher frequencies and consciousness become more available to you.

Your means of connection and communication are through vibration and resonance.
There's no communication across time and space when you resonate with something.
Instead, there's a mutual understanding,
A simultaneous sharing of consciousness,
A meeting and inhabiting of the same frequency.
This can occur when there's a conscious intention
Or a will to interact, liaise, co-mingle, and co-create experiences.

You will know how this feels when you connect with a fellow person in your life,
With whom you feel a rapport, an attraction, or an ease in being and communicating.
It feels comfortable,
And you are in active participation and willingness
To experience and share this relationship.
This feeling of connection can be there in your family
And the people you spend a lot of time with.

## Telepathic Communication

In learning to resonate with other things,
You may find that you can communicate telepathically with other Beings.
What we mean by this is that communication is non-physical.
While your language in this scenario may not be spoken,
The language used is vibrational.

In this sense, you are resonating and sharing consciousness with others,
Which means there can be a transfer of information.
But again, this is not a transportation of information through space and time
From one to the other:
It is an instantaneous, direct link established through a shared yet unseen field
That all minds have the potential to access.

Both parties in telepathic communication are tuned into a specific frequency,
Allowing them to sync-up and share information seamlessly.
Just as the airdrop on your phone doesn't require the data to physically travel
From one device to another,
Telepathic communication bypasses traditional sensory channels,
Offering a form of connection that is immediate and intimate,
As it involves the direct exchange of mental or emotional states
Without the need for words or gestures.
You may already be experiencing this with loved ones
And those you spend much time with.

Non-physical communication comes in many forms.
By being more integrated with your non-physical I AM Self
And living in more alignment,
You may better understand other people and experiences.

# Encounters Beyond Human Beings

We would like to talk to you now about this same thing
With beings that you do not recognise as human.
By this, we refer to other species,
Both of your planet and other planets, habitations and existences.
While some beings you connect with may enjoy physical experience,
Others may enjoy non-physical form and experience.

Many of you have or wish to have, this kind of connection
With the animals and plants of your world, including your pets.
Some of you experience connection with Beings from other realms of consciousness
That are physical or non-physical.
In any case, the common denominator with all of these possibilities is *consciousness.*
Because consciousness is the medium of All-That-Is,
That is holographic, containing all information and all beings within it.
It is the ultimate experience of God.

In your explorations of non-physical experience,
You may also experience consciousness from other versions of Self.
You may perceive these as Selves that are from the past or future.
They might also be what you regard as *current* or present-time beings,
Based on your concept and measurement of time.

A connection can enlighten you
And offer you development and growth in your journey through physical experience.
Remember, you are a channel of I AM energy.

However, you can also channel into your physical experience
That which you consciously exchange with other forms of God reflection.
By this, we mean *other* forms of being.

Although, you may not entirely understand your interpretation of this energy.
For example, you may experience this contact in ways your body or *whole being* can translate,
But your cognitive mind cannot.
Nevertheless, your intellect and imagination will do their best
To interpret this energy in presentable forms.

As the collective energy known as Tarp,
Our physical visual form is an abstraction,
Not something Gayle can accurately articulate.
She sometimes perceives us as a deep vortex of purple and blue light;
At other times, an indigo-purple cloud.
However, she always perceives us as a group or collective energy,
Unindividuated and devoid of individual characteristics like sex, age,
And other parameters you associate with humans.
What is evident in her perception is our *presence*.

The purpose of sharing how we manifest to Gayle
Is to illustrate how representations can emerge within your consciousness
Through the imaginal realm.
You receive these representations to interpret, translate, and integrate
Into your physical experience.
Understand that the intricate workings of these phenomena may seem beyond your grasp,
Especially while you strongly identify with your physical body.

Herein lies the profound role of the imaginal realm and your imagination,
Bridging this expansive understanding.
Imagination can translate energy into tangible, albeit imaginal, forms your mind can interpret.
Even when you can't find the right words to describe these manifestations,
Your mind processes and makes sense of them.

Remember that the representations you receive are just that:
Representations.
These beings' actual form and appearance might take a lot of work for you
To fully comprehend from your human perspective.
Nevertheless, *the vibrations are real*,
Representing the truth of these beings.
The frequency you share establishes the connection.
Your contact and communication are facilitated through these vibrations,
And this resonance is the ultimate truth.

As the entity known as Tarp,
We want to emphasise that during these encounters,
You might experience something familiar or something for which you already have a term,
Such as *Archangel Michael* or a *Pleiadian*.
However, you might also experience something partially recognisable,
Or something you can't fully comprehend or interpret.

Remember that the visual representation of what you are encountering
Is only surface-level,
Much like your physical appearance is a temporary manifestation of your physical Self
And doesn't indicate your Higher Self or God-Self.
Know that all beings are God-Beings, facets of the divine,
Manifesting or representing themselves to you
In ways that aid your connection and communication.

There is a mutual understanding of what certain archetypical beings look like.
For instance, there is a consensus on what an elephant looks like,
And through mass consciousness, representation and agreement,
There is a general understanding of who Jesus Christ appears to be.
This same principle applies to beings from other worlds, planes, and dimensions.
The shared agreements about these appearances aren't confined to individuals on your Earth,
But extend to different perspectives.

We're trying to convey that these visual appearances
Benefit your understanding and processing of the energy.
Still, the core truth lies within the vibration and frequency of energy,
As vibration precedes form.

We encourage you to foster a personal, experiential relationship with God,
That which *you* are, in physical form.
This relationship is cultivated through your daily consciousness and awareness of it.
Your loving action is akin to worship of this truth.
It is also a service to yourself and, simultaneously, all other Beings,
For you are all ultimately in union.

Your pursuit of good feelings or alignment with the I AM aligns with truth.
As you grow consciously and spiritually,
You will become more aligned with this inner divine presence,
And the influence of the I AM becomes more predominant
In guiding your decisions and actions.

# The Ultimate Relationship with God

Therefore, you are free to resonate with and choose your experience.
Still, the ultimate relationship to develop and cultivate is with God.
You can channel this, and you can channel *all* its forms of being.
However, your relationship with God is your purpose.
By relationship, we mean your connection to and your understanding of All-That-Is.

Therefore, even though other forms may feel like *other* or *alien* to you,
Know that all are actually One, and all originate from the same source.
And all connections with other forms of consciousness and being
Can be regarded as *Agents* for your connection to God,
Agents for your ascendance towards greater union with Self.

For each being has a unique and valuable role to play in the cosmic scheme of things.
This can be considered *spiritual development*;
The goal is to integrate your ego Self with the divine presence of I AM.
Through this integration, you will experience the full realisation of your divine potential.

CHAPTER

17

# Lessening the Differences

## The Perceived 'Other'

We encourage you to examine your reactions to what you perceive as *other* or different
In your immediate physical environment and daily experiences.
For observing difference and identifying this as truth,
Creates a feeling of separation within and around you.

Identifying something as different from you can happen in two ways:
Either you see something different to you and conclude that it is, therefore, different to you.
Or, you are free to perceive something as different to you,
But understand and acknowledge that it is the same essence and divine energy in another form,
And that both you and it spring from the same source.

*We are not asking you to ignore the differences.*
For distinguishing in your physical world is helpful to you.
Recognising differences in your world and throughout your physical life is a survival mechanism,
Aiding you in forming patterns, judgments, beliefs, and understanding about the world,
Its inhabitants, and phenomena.
This allows you to navigate your environment in time and space with discernment.

## Acknowledging Unity Amid Differences

However, now is an excellent time to take the consciousness of All-That-Is
Into your working, everyday consciousness.
As we have emphasised, this awareness enhances your connection to all facets of life.
This awareness, as we have said, is your connection that *dramatically* improves all of life.

It is a higher vibrational way of being,
To understand and practise in your life experience
That you, we and all Beings are of One essence.
We are *all* God,
Experiencing itself from different perspectives.

Knowing this, you can see that it is living out as creation intended,
Appreciating the diverse viewpoints and frequencies the Universe experiences,
Making your physical experience abundant, textured, engaging, and co-creative.
The sense and experience of *Self* and *other* is necessary to some extent,
As we've discussed regarding the ego,
Because it helps you move through your physical world.

However, the sense of Union and Being-ness from All-That-Is
Helps you to live your physical life with success:
Greater connectivity, perceptibility, consciousness, compassion, creativity,
Productivity and relatability.

This might seem straightforward as you read these words,
But we encourage you to reflect on it practically,
Considering those differences you have identified in your physical experience
That may be challenging to let go of.

## Uncovering Subconscious Beliefs

You may have deep-seated beliefs about differences you are unaware of.
Consider aspects of differing viewpoints such as race, religion, politics, and culture.
These beliefs can influence how you perceive others and interact with them.
You may hold rigid views about certain groups,
And believe that clinging to these notions or preconceptions will serve you well,
Keep you from harm, or uphold your values.

Similarly, fear or misconceptions about certain animals or situations can evoke anxiety.
Adjusting these perceptions and recognising your shared essence with these things
Can feel, not only daunting, but also as though it compromises your sense of security.
These deeply-ingrained beliefs can act as barriers to understanding,
Connection, empathy, and unity, reinforcing divisions
And the idea of separateness
Rather than celebrating shared humanity and interconnectedness.

Beliefs, mainly those deeply ingrained,
Often reside in the subconscious mind.
They operate like the background programming of your mind,
Influencing your thoughts, decisions, and reactions,
Without you necessarily being aware of them.

From early childhood, you absorb beliefs –
From your environment, family, culture, and personal experiences –
And these ideas become embedded in your subconsciousness.
Even as you grow and learn,
These subconscious beliefs shape your worldview, sense of Self, and interaction with others.

Consequently, understanding and transforming these subconscious beliefs
Requires deliberate introspection and conscious effort
To uncover what might otherwise remain hidden.
Your reason for wanting to uncover such ingrained beliefs and fears
Is so you can find more alignment and connection with All-That-Is.

For instance, you might believe that your fear of snakes keeps you safe,
As it encourages you to maintain a distance from them.
This belief might be so strong that you experience a physical reaction of fear
Upon encountering or even thinking about a snake.
This is crucial to understanding and putting into daily living the art of connection to All-that-Is.
The art of knowing and feeling the I AM of who you are,
Knowing the God you are of, and the God the other fearful thing, the snake, is also.
Interplaying in physical experience to represent and play out different viewpoints of experience,
But borne out of love all the same.

We know that overcoming these profoundly-ingrained fears and beliefs can be challenging.
We do not want you to feel pressure;
Just feel an awareness growing within, as though a seed has been planted
That you may one day entertain the idea that there is nothing really to be fearful of,
Because the snake is just a representation of god energy in different form,
And God energy is within you both,
Beyond and around you both,
Even after both your physical forms are gone.
Because ultimately, there is no death.

Remembering there is no death;
Remembering the eternal, unbreakable connection to God and All-That-Is
Means that if you do not fear death,
You will not fear harm from the snake.

This awareness of the non-physical I AM Self of who you are,
Combined and integrated with the sensory awareness of your ego-body complex,
Allows you to recognise yourself as distinct from others
To the degree that it helps you get things done,
Enables you to keep out of the way from harm,
Such as not going too near the poisonous snake,
But allows you to see the same aspect of God within the snake
That you know you have within yourself.

There is a lessening of the differences
In a way that keeps you functioning in the physical plane,
Yet connected to the non-physical realm
Without fear of death, because there is only union.

Therefore, try to lessen the differences you see among your fellow human being *God-Selves*,
And lessen the differences between the other animals and species of your planet.
Be vibration-oriented,
And make your action in the world *loving*:
With kindness, good intention, and well-being.

If you can lessen the differences among what you see
In your physical environment on your planet,
You are well on your way to being able to connect with,
And co-create your experience with, beings from beyond your physical dimension
And beyond your Earth.
However, outside your physical realm,
There are more considerable vibrational disparities to consider.
Still, resonance is possible.

As we have mentioned,
There are connections and resonances you may feel with certain beings
That make it easier than others for you to connect and channel.

Higher-frequency beings, with their clearer vantage points,
Have a more comprehensive understanding of how everything exists within the All.
They are able to reach down, vibrationally speaking,
To make a connection to you when you are in alignment with yourself
And feeling connected to your Higher Self.

They can adjust their vibrational frequency to connect with you
When you are in alignment with yourself and feeling connected to your Higher Self.
When your frequency rises, they can find a frequency platform or *common ground*
For your synchronisation to occur.
This adjustment in their frequency enables you to blend consciousness
To the degree you can understand.

Just as we merge our consciousness with Gayle to a degree that she can understand.
Note that she is not able to comprehend *all* of what our consciousness is,
But that is okay,
For she is comprehending just the perfect amount for what she can translate
And for you, the reader, to absorb.
And this process of frequency match and common ground with higher-frequency beings
Would be the same for you in *your* connection.

To illustrate this further:
Just as you can comprehend from a higher-consciousness vantage point
The lower vibrational beings in your world,
Such as certain species of animals, plants, or minerals,
As a human, with your creative mind, free will, and imagination,
You are better positioned to understand, help, and even oversee these beings.

Consider, for instance, a colony of ants.
You can observe and comprehend their entire ecosystem from a higher vantage point.
Still, they cannot understand *your* entire ecosystem.
Just as you may look down on them to see their whole interactions in life,
This is how higher-conscious beings may be able to understand you.

The higher the consciousness, the greater the awareness of All-That-Is,
And the stronger the connection to union they experience.
Every facet of existence is nested within each being.
You are able to comprehend what you have evolved through.

Therefore, a higher consciousness being will be able to perceive more of who you are
Than you can perceive of yourself!
Given that your physical life is unfolding in what seems to you to be a linear timeline
And all of it *as a whole* is yet to be apparent to you.

Higher consciousness beings will understand you from a whole perspective,
Rather than a splintered-off, compartmentalised ego-body, complex perspective.

## Connecting with Higher Consciousness

Hence, when contact happens with such Beings,
Your interpretation comes in a comprehensive form through your imagination –
Through the non-physical imaginal realm.

You might not fully grasp how to process this, interpret it, or reach out to them.
However, you can recognise the unity of All-That-Is,
And set a loving intention for connection.
If your goal is to connect with a higher-consciousness being,
Specifically set your intention to align with this higher consciousness,
And practice this connection in your everyday life.

The more you engage with this connection,
With loving action and loving intention,
The higher your vibration will rise and the more you will understand.
The more you will understand, the less you will fear.
The less you fear, the more coherent and integrated you will be.

Understanding enhances your resonance with higher frequencies
And higher-frequency consciousness,
As well as with the Beings within this higher realm.
This process of continual growth, expansion, and deepening awareness
Enables you to bridge the gap between your current conscious state
And the higher realms of existence.

Remember, all beings, including you, are manifestations of the same divine Source energy,
Experiencing itself in myriad forms.
Embracing this understanding fosters connection, compassion, and oneness,
Transforming your perspective of Self, others, and the Universe.

You may experience visual differences,
But underneath it, all is a complete union.

CHAPTER

18

# Falling Down, Picking Yourself Up Again

## The Gradual Integration

All of this we have communicated is to help you integrate
The fullness of Who-You-Are more smoothly into your life.
To integrate and embody during your space-time experience on Earth.

It is a process that will absorb and awaken within you gradually,
In accordance and alignment with your readiness.
While you already know all of this on one level of consciousness
And can see where someone else is not putting this into practice,
There might be resistance to incorporating these insights into *your* understanding of being.

## Understanding the Space-Time Discrepancy

There may be moments when you feel you've grasped the essence of these teachings.
Still, your physical life doesn't seem to be working out for you,
And your physical life doesn't seem to align with this understanding.
Sometimes, your observations of the physical world might not reflect your internalised wisdom.
Remember that the physical realm is constantly playing catch-up to the non-physical.
For it is an after-projection of the non-physical vibration.

We encourage you to trust in your knowing.
The greater your alignment and awareness of Oneness to All-That-Is,
The narrower the interval between your desires and their physical manifestations will become.
This alignment is not just an intellectual exercise,
But a vibration orientation of your life.

For you, it is a practical and comprehensive living and experiencing
That will allow you to notice the results.
When this begins to happen more and more,
When you start to integrate this into your being,
And as you deepen this understanding,
Your experience of the temporal and spatial gap between what you transmit vibrationally,
And the desires of your life with their physical appearance in your life, will minimise.
You would be experiencing, in other words, more remarkable *synchronicity*.
A life where you quickly notice the relationship
Between that which you are transmitting vibrationally,
And that which you are having mirrored back to you by All-That-Is.

Experience to you would seem more connected,
And you may perceive the collapsing of the lag between cause-and-effect,
Aspirations and their manifestations.
This plays out as a tangible mirror –
Something you can recognise, reflecting your vibrational alignment to you
And providing a more immediate, synchronistic feedback loop in your physical existence.

However, even when you become better at attracting
The higher vibrational frequencies of those things you desire,
Because you are resonating the frequency equivalent to those things,
You will still experience a *lag* in your time-space existence.

This is the nature of your physical existence.
Here, with your life on Earth,
Your experience is framed within the parameters of space and time.
You cannot move in space without time passing,
And you cannot experience time passing without moving in space.
Even if you stayed completely still,
Because experiencing the passing of time changes your environment's configuration.

Your Earth orbits the sun, and everything in your cosmos, even at the quantum level,
Is in a constant state of motion,
Imperceptible to human senses or not.
These are anchor points in which your physical body form
And accompanying sensory experience, or normal waking state, is bound.

Nevertheless, even though it will not be eliminated entirely while you are in a physical experience,
Closing this gap is a wonderful achievement.
Because it is a joy to see the flow of transmission and receiving in smaller cycles.
Witnessing your desires manifest more quickly after setting your intention,
And leading your life vibrationally oriented can bring immense satisfaction.
Seeing things show up in your life shortly after you have been thinking about them,
As well as beginning to see patterns and repetitions, is exhilarating.
All of this is life-affirming and confidence-building.

As your intuition becomes more potent,
Your sense of who you are and what is better for you develops,
Meaning you are better at aligning yourself,
Giving you an integrated and wholesome perspective on Earth.
This will keep you on a content and fulfilling life path.

Trust in your power and connection to All-That-Is to manifest and shape your reality.
This isn't just about attracting what you desire into your life,
But also about becoming more in tune with who you truly are,
And living a life that reflects that authenticity.

## Breaking Free from Denser Vibration

However, sometimes things will not go right.
You will not feel okay,
And things may not seem to be going your way.
You may feel a struggle,
Or get caught up in worries and denser emotions like anger and despair.
By *denser*, we refer to vibrations that resonate at lower frequencies.

These emotional states are termed *dense*
Because they carry a heavier, slower vibration,
Compared to emotions such as joy or love,
Which are associated with higher, lighter frequencies.

Such lower vibrations can often cause discomfort, struggle,
Or the perception that things are not aligning in your favour,
With the intensity of your emotions creating a seemingly impenetrable barrier
Between you and the rest of the world.

When these incidents happen,
You feel as if you are alone in your suffering,
And it becomes a very private matter;
Even if you share with another,
The sense and density of your emotions are such
That you believe you and you alone are going through it,
And someone else cannot understand how you feel.

Here, you feel disconnected, and during these times,
It's essential to understand that you've seemingly lost the *feeling* of connection
To your non-physical Self that you truly are.
Instead, you have become overly identified with the smaller ego self,
And caught up in a negatively fulfilling feedback loop that perpetuates your pain.

In other words, you are manifesting the proof that your negative belief about yourself
And the situation is correct.
It might feel strangely good to you to confirm your belief (whatever it is).
*Good* in a small way, because by making yourself right in those situations,
You listen to the small Self's ideas of survival,
That you will be safe if you observe what it is telling you.

There is a subconscious motivation to feel and believe this way
Because it will serve you on some level,
Perhaps by keeping you safe,
Avoiding disappointment, rejection, greater pain or suffering.

Why does this happen?
This is a survival strategy.
Yet, while this loop might serve you on some level,
It ultimately keeps you stuck in a lower vibrational frequency.

In vibrational terms, you transmit a denser, heavier energy that is harder to shift.
Its resonance attracts similar vibrational frequency,
And it's as if you have created a magnet that pulls in experiences that match this lower frequency,
Resulting in a negative feedback loop.

By *negative feedback loop*, we mean a recurring cycle,
Where your lower, denser energy frequencies attract similar energy vibrations,
Leading to the repetition of undesirable experiences,
Further reinforcing the initial lower vibrations,
And your negative beliefs create a continuous cycle of negativity.
This can make it feel easier to stay stuck rather than break free.

As you may be aware in the physics of your physical world,
The denser the matter, the stronger the gravitational pull.
The same principle applies to the non-physical world of vibration and attraction –
Though you might think of it more as magnetism than gravity.

## Restoring That Feeling of Oneness and Wholeness in the Midst of Delusion

So, during these challenging times,
Remember that you're experiencing a lower vibrational state.
Understanding this can be the first step towards shifting your energy
And breaking free from the negative feedback loop.

Remember that when you find yourself in a state of discomfort, feeling lost or stuck,
The path to resolution lies in re-establishing the connection with your true Self,
The essential *I AM* of your being.

A practical way to do this is to enter your environment.
We ask you to *step out* into the environment around you,
Look around your world and deliberately and actively find other Being-ness,
Plants, flowers, minerals, animals, and humans,
And gaze upon them.

Look for beauty and diversity.
Engage in wonder at your world,
And with loving action (passive or active).
For these are your other *nodes* of Self.
These are the other *nodes* of God,
*Your* essence, experiencing itself.

Think of this Oneness as having many tentacles,
Feeling into the experience from different vantage points.
The root of these tentacles is the same root for all.
The same basis, the same origin. The same source.
Therefore, if you are not feeling good within your physical Self,
Look to the other aspects of God, for you are One with them.
You can enjoy your imagination to feel and resonate with this manifestation around you.

As you gaze at another type of being,
Understand that the object of your focus,
Be it a blade of grass or a human,
Possesses an inherent awareness of its identity as a manifested form of energy.

A blade of grass knows it is a blade of grass.
Yet, behind all these individual perspectives lies a unifying understanding of Oneness and Unity.
We ask you in these times of less alignment to look at these things,
And they will soothe you and lift you up.

So, when you feel like you have *fallen down,*
Venture into your surrounding world and focus upon another manifestation of being.
In doing so, you affirm the truth of your interconnectedness.
You are part of the physical world, and simultaneously part of the God Source,
Intertwined with all the other forms you perceive around you.
You are the I AM!
While simultaneously, you are all that you see!
We remind you that you are a holographic being in a holographic Universe:
Every form of energy, manifested or unmanifested, imaginable or beyond comprehension,
Is part of you, as you are part of it.

All faces of love and aspects of God in the Universe are within you,
Folded into your being,
Just as they are within every other being you observe.
You are One with all.

Therefore, feelings of separation are merely temporary illusions,
Momentary forgetfulness of your true nature.
These feelings of separateness are not *real,*
Because they are not permanent and do not reflect the ultimate truth of your being.

In moments of discomfort or struggle, remember this essential Oneness,
And use it as a compass to guide you back to a state of harmony and connection.
Look for a way to feel at ease.
This is about shifting your mind and steering your focus away
From the mechanistic patterns of your ego,
Its motives and belief systems,
To keep you in survival mode or *action-orientation.*

By this, we mean acting without conscious awareness of your feelings,
And without deliberate intention to feel better things.
The mind can act in self-fulfilling ways,
Seeking to prove that your beliefs are correct.

However, this part of the mind and ego functions from past and future analysis,
Rather than from conscious awareness in the present.
These patterns can hinder your connection to the more expansive,
vibrationally-oriented awareness of your true Self.

## Practical Steps for Realigning

On a practical level, consider engaging in activities that will anchor you in the present moment,
To distract the ego and quieten the mental chatter.
Typically, your worries and anxieties are grounded in your perceptions of the past and future.
Still, these temporal dimensions do not truly exist as you think they do.
Only the present is real,
So engaging in activities that bring you back to the *now* can be a powerful tool
For reconnecting with the I AM frequency you are.

There are many ways to shift your focus and move beyond your cognitive circuitry.
These methods generally involve activities that occupy your mind,
Distracting you from your negative-feeling loop,
And disrupting the automatic thinking habits,
To raise your vibration and bring about a feeling of ease.

This state of flow, often associated with activities that demand your full attention,
Can lead to an altered state of consciousness.
In this channeling state, you are channeling more of who you are
And your natural unique frequency,
Which feels comfortable, easy, and aligned.
It is where the non-physical I AM can flow through you.

The goal is to *be* rather than to *do*,
To experience as a vibrational being, integrated with the physical body,
Rather than engaging in actions from a place of vibrational detachment.
The activities that can facilitate this process are varied.

Some may be predominantly left-brained activities,
Which engage analytical and logical thinking.
Others may be right-brained activities,
Associated with creativity and holistic thinking.
Some activities may engage both sides of the brain simultaneously.

As you distract yourself and engage in something occupying your mind,
You allow more of the non-physical I AM into your physical presence.
This process helps you resonate once again with your unique vibrational frequency,
Bringing you into greater alignment, peace, and well-being.

Serving others is another powerful method for reconnecting with the I AM,
For it takes you out of self-ego-centred thought patterns,
And enables a reestablishment of loving actions.
The energy of service is circular; as you give love, you receive it in return,
Reaffirming your unity with All-That-Is.

# Returning to Unanimity and Affinity

However, we remind you that you never lose connection,
For it is always there.
*Falling down* is only an illusion of falling down,
And it can never be permanent, for this is impossible.
The consciousness of the I AM remains,
Even when you feel separated from it because it is eternal.

The ego and mind are loyal, functional tools for navigating life's physical, space-time experience.
Still, when you become overly identified with them,
You risk mistaking them for your true Self.
When this happens, you become vulnerable to the ups and downs of physical existence,
With your value attached to action and reaction rather than vibration.
The ego mind, while useful, is not the totality of who you are.

You are always more than you believe yourself to be;
You are boundless and free.
The physical ego-body complex merely guides you through the physical plane.
The goal is not to reject or suppress the ego and mind,
But to integrate it with the non-physical, the I AM.

To harmonise these two aspects of your being,
You can move through this world,
*Realised* in physical and spiritual potential.
This integration will lead to profound joy and fulfilment in your physical experience.

CHAPTER

19

# The Merging of the Two into One

# Delighting in the Duality of Your Trans-Physical Experience

You move through a landscape filled with contrast and polarity in the physical world.
By *polarity*, we refer to phenomena of opposing pairs.
You will experience light and dark, hot and cold, masculine and feminine, joy and pain,
And all blends, grades and varieties in between.

These pairs of binary opposites, intrinsic to your physical world,
Give you matter to move towards and repel away from.
Just like a battery:
The functioning of the battery operates on the principles of positive and negative charges
To generate energy and power.

These opposites are essential for manifesting energy and movement in a physical world.
They are forces that attract and repel,
Much like the opposing phenomena in your life,
Creating a dynamic interplay fundamental to life's existence and experience.

We would like to emphasise that this duality in your experience
Is not just about witnessing a state of conflict or tension,
But rather a necessary condition for the *flow* and *transformation* of energy,
Not just in your physical life, but in the physical Universe.

You can expect this range of contrast and polarity in your life,
Because it is inherent in physical existence and natural to human experience.
It provides a framework, allowing you to define and understand your unique path.
It gives you points of reference among the illusion of infinite manifestation
In a linear, space-time way.

This fantastic diversity facilitates sequential experiences,
And enables you to grow, learn from, and explore.
Depending on your preferences,
They provide the experience for you to be attracted to or repelled by things.

However, there is an *art* to living in this kind of binary physical experience,
Which is to find *equilibrium* between the polarities.
In other words, embrace the duality, but work on viewing it all with *equanimity.*

Notice the contrast, but try to avoid getting pulled out of alignment with it.
Understanding the impermanence of everything you come across,
Not just the unpleasant but also the good things, cultivates that sense of equanimity.
Others may refer to it as non-attachment.
But we encourage you to *feel* things for the sake of feeling:
To be vibration-conscious.

## Mastering the Art of Living in Accord with All-That-Is

*To explain more:* If you are looking for higher vibration phenomena in your world,
It is not really for the acquisition of the phenomena,
But rather the higher vibrational consciousness that you think it will bring.
In other words, your desire to look for things that feel good to you in your world
Is not so you can have the *things* that feel good (although you may think it is).
It is so you can have *feelings* that feel good.

This subconscious motivation is your non-physical *internal compass,*
Trying to bring you back to the natural state of harmony and joy.
After all, your ultimate freedom comes from realising the Oneness and union
Of everything in All-That-Is.
You are eternal and transcendent –
Even in this contrasting, compelling, physical experience you are in.

Another duality you will experience in your physical life
Is the functioning of the two hemispheres of your brain,
Which are inherently dualistic in structure and function.
Each brain hemisphere is specialised:
The left hemisphere is adapted for logical, analytical, and language-related processing.
The right hemisphere is more involved in creative, intuitive, and holistic thinking.

The two aspects are a necessary and natural balance,
Allowing a full and rich human experience.
They exist and work in tandem to provide a complete range of cognitive and perceptual abilities.
Finding integration and harmony in function between the two hemispheres is ideal.

However, you may generally fall into a left-brain dominance in ego and mind
With how it functions in your world.
We encourage you to balance the analytical, linear thinking of the left brain
With the creative, holistic awareness of the right brain.

Engage in activities that challenge both sides of your brain,
Fostering harmony and integration between these distinct yet complementary modes of mind.
There are practical exercises that will cultivate this, and help you to experience more harmony.

We also encourage you to embrace the masculine and feminine qualities of energy,
And find harmony with the two,
For with one aspect and not the other,
You will not realise your wholeness and perfection.

Through all pairs of opposites you come across, we encourage you to find harmony.
Acknowledge, understand, embrace, and use your divine integrated identity
To harmonise all you see within your life.
You can master your reactions to your contrasting experiences
By being vibration-oriented.
Instead of letting the contrast that you see
And consequently, your reactions to them dictate how your life should be,

Master the art of living, merge the two (contrasts) into One,
Realise the unified source of everything,
And let your vibration steer your choices of how your life should be.

We encourage you to merge your internal world with your external world,
Keeping your awareness and focus on who you are and your experience's contrasting nature.
We would like you to praise and celebrate the union of All-That-Is
And the unique manifestation energy streams of all you come across in the Universe.

You see, all of creation is in relationship with itself.
There *is* opposition,
And there *is also* union.
Both are necessary to understand the truth of itself.

We offer words of comfort that, even in those moments when you perceive darkness,
There is always a light, a spark of divine consciousness, waiting to guide you.
In times of struggle or perceived *downfall*,
Remember that you are never truly lost.
You are an eternal being, an individuated expression of God's energy,
Navigating the dualities of physical existence.

Behind all *being-ness*, positive and negative,
And anything you perceive as unfavourable,
Ultimately, there is only love.
That from love, there are actings out of the pairs of opposites
Serving as an archetype, precipitator or catalyst for change, flow, realisation and enlightenment.
So that you may grow, experience, and return to love.
And know the ultimate truth and experience that is God.
*You are not alone*.

Each interaction, each relationship, and each experience
Offers a new perspective, a new angle, and a new dimension of the divine.
All of the polarity you experience is there to help your realisation,
For the joy of experiencing,
So that consciousness or God may encounter more of itself.

Be at peace with this, for you are held in so much love.
In a landscape of contrast, Small Self, remember who you are.

# Allowing Your Energy to Flow Through You

## Discovering Your Holistic Purpose

Now, we want to reflect on having a *purpose* in life.
We understand that it is a question you ask,
And a popular topic from time to time in your physical world.
We do not wish to confuse you with words,
But the *objective* is to express your unique energy in physical form.

When we say *purpose*, however, we do not wish you to get hung up on your goal beyond that:
We do not wish you to take your *purpose* too seriously.
Instead, we would like you to acknowledge, understand and accept who you are holistically.

Your objective is not about achieving specific goals or missions in the traditional sense.
Instead, it is about integrating and expressing your higher I AM Self
With your earthly Self, the small, ego Self.
You serve this objective by understanding and keeping in mind your connection
And awareness of who you are.
By integrating the two aspects of Self into your life,
Therefore, your *purpose*, as such,
Is to let your energy flow through you into your physical world.

In essence, you are an eternal divine being having a temporary human experience,
And your *purpose* is to express and experience that divinity in the physical world.

Thus, live in the present moment,
And feel the connection and vibration of all experiences!

Maintain, as much as you can, an orientation through life,
According to how it feels, vibrationally speaking.
Living with this integrated understanding means staying connected and aware
As much as possible in the present moment,
And tuning into the vibrational essence of your experiences,
Rather than solely relying on intellectual analysis or societal expectations to guide your actions.

Turn your attention inward to your internal vibration,
Your intuitive guidance system.
Actively seek experiences that uplift you and resonate with your inner being.
Your emotions are a vital feedback system,
Guiding you toward what feels right and away from what doesn't.

The Universe is an energetic mirror,
Reflecting the energy you emit through your thoughts, emotions, and actions.
Become masterful over your vibrational transmission
And enjoy receiving the experience reflected back to you from this energy-based All-That-Is.

This is not about ignoring your thoughts or denying your bodily experiences.
On the contrary, it's about harmonising your physical existence with your non-physical essence.
It's about becoming a master of your energy and vibration,
While harnessing your physical senses, cognitive abilities, and body as a vehicle
For experiencing and interacting with the world.
Therefore, we encourage you to take care of your physical body,
As it is the perfect accommodation for your I AM Self.

You have the capacity for joy, learning, growth, passion.
Remember, your life's journey is not a test or a race, but a dance through polarity.
It's a creative exploration, where the objective is not to arrive at a specific destination,
But to delight in each step, each movement, and each moment.
The journey for *journey's* sake.
And to find that balance.

## Contributing to the Infinite Heavenly Realisation

Regularly remind yourself of your true identity and purpose;
Living from that integrated space can transform your life.
It brings a deeper sense of peace and fulfilment as you align with your authentic being
That channels and expresses your unique energy.

Your awareness and connection to the two Selves
Can bring you so much happiness and success.
It is absolutely worth reminding yourself to be and live your life like this,
Until it becomes a habit.

Your unique energy stream is a precious and essential part of All-That-Is!
Just by being you, by being present and aligned with your I AM essence,
You are fulfilling a *divine purpose*.

Your thoughts, feelings, words, and actions
Have far-reaching implications beyond yourself.
They contribute to the collective consciousness,
Impact other beings,
And shape the fabric of your shared reality.

Therefore, consciously try to experience by 'Being' (*being* in the moment and feeling)
Before action or *doing*.
Although doing is necessary in your physical world,

Remember that the nature of your being is to conduct this energy
And stream it into your life experience.
Your unique energy stream creates a unique expression in your life.
Think of your life as the canvas where you can paint the picture of the life you desire.
It will change, and you will change your life creation repeatedly,
According to what you feel.

Your life path will have unique experiences, creations, conversations, thoughts and ideas
As you go along your way.
The result is original, divine, meaningful, and valuable to All-That-Is.
For what you do in your life and how you think, feel, and act
Affects everything else around you most beautifully.
Everything you do contributes to how other Beings experience and act in *their* life.

The eternal energy of other God-streams, or I AMs in human form,
Continuously interact and co-create with you in an ever-moving,
Yet divinely wholesome and perfect way.

So, you are a face of God in a physical world,
Participating with billions of other streams of I AM, *also* in physical form.
You are *all* part of the One,
But all with an individual viewpoint, focus, expression, identity, personality,
And contribution to your world.

Whether you are meeting everyone in the world (which you won't) or not,
Your experiences still influence each other.
Therefore, apart from living your life *being* and knowing who you are,
Let this energy flow through you!

Allowing this unique flow is *love-in-action*.
It is channeling the source of Who-You-Are and All-That-Is through you into the physical world.
Your actions, experiences, and *everything* you do create resonance.
Your awareness enables you to participate actively in this grand cosmic dance of creation.

So, embrace your unique essence, and remember that you are an integral part of the All-That-Is,
Continuously contributing to the divine tapestry of existence,
With every moment of your being.
Therefore, following what makes you feel good is *righteous* for you
And the world around you,
Because it is in sync with creation and All-That-Is.

Yours is a valuable role to play,
No matter what measure of significance your small Self may think it has.
Do not worry about what others think.
Doing what resonates well with you and feels good
Is the best thing you can do for yourself.
*No one else will know better than you when you feel aligned and connected with your Higher Self.*

You may feel that this can sound Selfish,
But it is a profound act of alignment with the divine.
Your life is akin to a prayer.
Because when you honour your true Self and act in alignment with your highest good,
You also contribute to the highest good of all.

The more happiness you feel,
The more love, connection and well-being you will feel and channel into the world.
Allow your energy to flow through, and know this is your purpose.
This is a valuable learning lesson we would like you to understand.
The more you let this energy flow through you,
The more you will realise that you are in union with All-That-Is.

Each person you encounter is on their own journey,
With their own experiences, perceptions, and beliefs that inform their responses.
Remembering this when met with cynicism, criticism, fear, or doubt is essential.
Do not let this bother you, for all beings can feel temporary disconnection occasionally.

Some people feel it more, or for more extended periods than others.
These reactions are more reflective of the individual's internal state than about you.
Recognise who they are and understand the process for humans in physical form,
Which is to go through these moments of contrast,
And use them to learn from and seek out the best path.

All streams of life have their own unique path:
Different journeys, different stories, different experiences, expressions and frequencies.
Here, understanding and compassion are vital.
It can be helpful to see beyond the immediate reaction,
Lessen the differences you see,
And recognise the divine essence within them.
This will enable you to feel empathy, even in challenging situations.

Your path is your own.
Allow your energy to flow through you.
This is your objective and *purpose.*

CHAPTER 21

# Using Channeling for Personal Growth

The ego tends to forget the source of where it is energised and where it has originated.
Because the ego and the working part of the mind
Try to manage the environment of contrasts.

In its quest to safeguard your physical existence,
The ego tends to perceive itself as separate from the rest of existence.

However, while this may be crucial for your physical preservation,
It compartmentalises your psyche,
Leading to a segregated way of perceiving phenomena.
It can suppress and invalidate experiences with non-physical experience, too.
This means it can inhibit your understanding of the non-physical realm.

However, the other side of the mind,
Which is linked to a less analytical, more flowing consciousness,
Also helps by providing intuition.
Sometimes, this guidance manifests as a gut feeling,
Something gleaned from a dream, or an intuitive hunch.

As a species, you have embraced both sides of this kind of living,
And have a dual modality of existence.
Balancing the left and right sides of the brain,
The small (ego) Self and the I AM Self.

However, in your current world,
Your experience has tilted towards a more left-sided way of navigating your life journey.
This approach involves egocentric actions, thoughts, expressions, decisions, and behaviours.
By *egocentric actions*, we mean they tend to be more action-oriented,
Governed by the ego and the small Self,
And less informed by the feeling of vibration or the connection to the I AM Self.

We refer to those actions motivated by the sense of separation or fear,
Analysing and strategising,
Driven by the ambition to gain advantage or avoid harm.
These actions are often guided by past experiences or future anxieties,
And less by the intuitive feelings originating from a connection with the larger *I AM* Self.

The subconscious self-fulfilling mechanism of fear
Is at the root of many ego-driven behaviours.
Fear, in its many forms, underpins many of your responses to life situations.
Fear of loss, rejection, inadequacy, or the unknown
Is a powerful motivator that often triggers your most instinctual, egocentric reactions.

This fear-based mode of living disconnects you from the present moment,
The *only* actual reality,
And distances you from the higher, All-That-Is truth.
It tends to be more action-oriented and less informed by vibrational feelings
Or connection to the I AM Self.
Being aware of this is helpful.

Merge the two (aspects of Self) into the One wholeness of being.

If you can allow your Divine, God-Self, I AM energy to flow through you and on,
Out into the world through your actions,
You will develop and enlighten yourself and find mastery over your emotions.
You will feel more balanced, self-assured and confident in your being.

CHAPTER

22

# The Everyday Occurrence of Channeling

## The Act of Channeling Divine Energy

Letting this divine energy flow through you is the act of channeling.
It is bringing the unmanifest into your physical world,
Aligning with your Higher Self, being of higher frequency,
Resonating with an aspect of consciousness in the Universe,
And filtering it into your world to be used by you or others.
It is the act of letting frequency show you your path through physical life,
Which is helpful to you.

Channeling is a natural principle of energy transfer,
Akin to downloading intelligence from the broader field of consciousness
Beyond your human working mind.
You can think of this broader field of consciousness as being around you and within.

Your access comes via your vibrational transmission,
Resulting in an energy or data transfer that you can draw into your life.
Your interpretation of it is as unique as you are.
This is what you may think of as *creativity*,
And how humans produce an incredible array of output,
From art to medicine, intellectual to physical property, projects and assets.
Because each one of you has a unique way of transducing.

Yes, this is what you are: a powerful channel and transducer!

In everyday life, you constantly do this:
Transforming sensory information from both the outside and inside.
You also transform this energy into internal experiences and external actions.
Just as transducers convert energy from one form to another,
Facilitating interaction with and understanding of the world around them.
It is innate and what it means to be human.

However, we would like to emphasise that you translate energy *both* ways:
You take non-physical phenomena (energy, consciousness)
And translate it into physical things (via actions in your world).

You also do the reverse:
You take the physical things you encounter in your world
And translate them into the non-physical phenomena (via thoughts, feelings, vibrations).

Knowing this, we encourage you
To deliberately channel your energy into your physical experience,
*Especially* when it feels good.
This is *loving action* in the world.

These are the things that you think, feel, create, produce,
And anything that feels amazing that you project into your life
And express through your actions and to other beings.
Because you are in perfect harmony, alignment, acquiescence and connection,
When you draw into the physical world, the consciousness of All-That-Is.

Channeling doesn't necessarily require contact with another being.
It can be enlightenment that comes via any number of ways that resonate with you.
You may not even be conscious of it,
But there are states of channeling that can make you feel *at one*
With the activity you're engaged in.

Have you ever experienced a moment where you felt completely absorbed in an activity,
Feeling a sense of peace and harmony?
How did that make you feel?
This is channeling.

*Being conscious* that you are a channel
Acknowledges the integration of the I AM with your physical Self.
While it may sound extraordinary, given your cultural norms and connotations,
Channeling is intrinsic and natural.
It is your human nature.

We are reframing the concept to make it more understandable in your current, evolving life.
The idea may seem fantastic.
However, *you are* fantastic, divine Beings of Light,
Manifested into physical form for action in a physical world.
Thus, awareness and acknowledgement of what you are will expand your consciousness,
Which is less constrained and more integrated.

## The Everyday Occurrence of Channeling

Energy transfer may happen in various forms,
Resulting in thought, feeling, inspiration, intuition, instinct.
It can be expressed through your actions,
Such as talking, writing, painting, drawing, inventing, teaching, playing, and moving.

Direct channeling of communication from another being
May come to you via your spoken word or writing.
However, you may realise that the medium used before it appears as an expression,
Is *imagination*.

Your approach or expression to this is personal,
And indicated by your desires, interests, and passions.
Essentially, the things that make you feel good.

Your imagination serves as the bridge
Between expanded consciousness and your cognitive mind.
The consciousness or intelligence will assume the easiest way for your interpretation
Through the senses and body.
Remember, nothing comes from nowhere;
Everything comes from somewhere,
And that somewhere is everywhere.

We don't mean to sound cryptic,
But it's essential to understand that all is within and around you.
The key to making sense of this is to feel what feels good to you,
And choose to align as much as possible with the things that resonate well with you.

This is your light path and how you live and navigate day-to-day experiences.
You are in a vibration-based experience,
Where everything can be assessed according to your resonance.

Imagination and channeling are inherent to the human experience.
You wouldn't be human without these.

We reiterate, although your experience in this physical body is temporary,
Your I AM-ness will never cease.
We want you to understand just how powerful you are as a participant in your physical life.

The human brain, a hub of electrical circuitry,
Operates with non-physical energy flowing through it,
A presence beyond the physical.
The presence of the divine is the life force of your physical form.

You are in constant flow and streaming of this unique energy stream.
This flow is yours.
Yet consciousness and love of All-That-Is is to be shared by all beings in creation.

You are free to cut off your divine flow if you choose.
By *cut off*, we mean *denying* the divine flow of I AM Self,
For it cannot really be cut off, because it is eternal.
This denying is often unconsciously done through consistent identification with egocentric living.

Denying yourself in this way can come from over-emphasising the Self as separate,
And prioritising fear-based responses.
Together, they create a self-imposed barrier to the continual stream of divine energy,
Within and around you.

We say *barrier*, but we would prefer you to look at it as a *curtain*:
Something that you are able to easily move aside
To let the boundless flow come abundantly through again.
Your divine flow is always constant, and focused *entirely* upon you.

The more you know this, the more empowered you will feel by your I AM-ness.
This supply is endless.
The more you realise that abundant love and higher energy are yours,
The more instrumental you can become in shaping, crafting, and influencing the physical world
And experiences around you.

The more you merge the I AM with the physical experience,
Blending the two for the sake of unique expression,
The more you can participate deliberately in the act of biological life
As a *light* being or as a *God-being*.
The more you can navigate the waves of experience
And actively follow your path of what feels good to you.

## As Gayle Channels: A Blending of Consciousness

As we channel these words through Gayle,
She sits peacefully with her fingers poised over her laptop,
Feeling steady happiness as she streams a more expanded consciousness
Than when she is unaware.

She's seated in a park under a tree while she composes this passage,
Resonating blissfully with us.
Her frequency has risen and harmonises with our consciousness or energy stream.
Together, we are coherent and have found common ground
To communicate and exchange intelligence or consciousness.

Gayle experiences a feeling of coherence.
Her mind is quite clear.
She feels content and relaxed and is breathing softly with a low heartrate.
She is in harmonious alignment, feeling peace and balance.

We understand her body-mind complex more holistically than she does herself,
Or at least more than her *ego* self knows,
As our perception is expanded while hers is compartmentalised.

While she sits and registers the sounds of the park around her,
Her connection with us remains.
She experiences a blending of these two experiences *simultaneously*.
Her focus on the outside world is non-specific.
Instead, her sensory perception is heightened with her eyes closed,
And she aligns with the I AM Self.

As she channels our consciousness more frequently,
She grows more fluid and comfortable with our energy,
And its expression through her body and mind.
Sometimes, our communication is expressed verbally through her;
Other times, like now, it is conveyed in writing.
Yet other times, it is expressed through her hands,
When she can place them near or on another person for energy exchange.

Our communication is instant.
There is no waiting to see or hear words.
There is an instant sharing of consciousness that Gayle deciphers
Through her understanding of language and her world.

Like you, she also accesses broader forms of information,
Communication, and consciousness during sleep.
However, just like you, these are typically compartmentalised in her waking state,
To allow for ease of navigation during her day.
The entirety of her body and being possess an innate understanding of connection
To her larger non-physical Self.
Yet, her working mind doesn't interpret the energy of the *whole*.

Currently, she has intentionally connected with us to continue writing this book.
Soon, she will disengage and live her life without actively seeking to channel our consciousness.
For she needs to experience her physical world, too.
When she does this, her life takes on a greater sense of wholeness,
With moments when she recognises our information is seeping in during a conversation,
Or while driving her car, for instance.

She is finding an increasing blend between her normal mind and small self ego,
With the larger I AM of who she is.
This comforts her, and she is learning to keep this awareness more actively in her life.

As a result, she finds more synchronicity in her experience,
As she allows this energy to flow through her body.
She experiences increased connection, peace, and joy.
This is inevitable!
Because the greater the connection you cultivate with your Higher Self,
And the more you become aware of your channeling,
The more divine energy and higher consciousness stream into your life.

Divine One, *you are supernatural*:
Capable of drawing in and bringing through you God consciousness,
To be made manifest into your physical world.
All for the joy of creation, expansion, experience and enlightenment.

We wish you to effortlessly align with and accept your Divinity.
You stand prepared to embark on this new way of life.

CHAPTER

23

# Healing is Channeling

Healing is channeling.
Now, you may understand more readily that All-That-Is resides within you,
And your ability to channel into your physical world
Is entirely within your capabilities.

Healing is a suitable word to describe the easing of yourself
And reclamation of your well-being
From whatever diseased or maladapted form your mind and body complex presents.
Remember you have a natural inclination to stream energy from the non-physical realm
Into your Physical world.
This is an unstoppable process.
Even if you are not aware of it, or deny it.

However, with awareness, you will become more accepting
Of the dual nature of your experience in the physical body.
You are becoming more aware of the I AM you are,
And your union and connection to All-That-Is.
You are this, you are that.
You are both simultaneously.

With increasing integration over time,
You will understand your power over your physical experience.
The power of your thoughts, words, and actions.

We understand that, while in this physical experience,
It is easy to identify with the physical world and take that as the truth,
It is easy to allow what you see around you
(which is the manifestation that has followed vibration),
And let that inform you of how to be.

We understand that this physical world is convincing and distracting.
We know that the physical you with an ego comes with strong identifiers:
A name, an appearance, a personality, an address, a job, friends and family –
And all societal and cultural constructs that keep you attached
To the momentum of the physical world that you are in.
These attachments serve you and your experience in the physical world.

However, remember that despite these dressings, labels and accessories applied
To your physical Self and life,
You are much more.
You are God in a focused physical form
For the joy and expansion of experience.

If you can sustain this awareness, you will be able to understand
That you are actively and constantly manifesting in physical experience.
You are reestablishing yourself and generating your life in *every* moment.
This means you are also pulling into your physical Self the idea of sickness or health.

All is possible in the non-physical realm:
When you can conceive it and think of it, you begin to focus it on being.
Things become physical reality if they are focused on and believed.

This principle applies to all kinds of phenomena and experiences in your life.
This also applies to healing:
The idea of health, wellness and the healing
Of that which displeases you in your physical experience.
You can heal yourself in whatever capacity you wish
And to what degree you believe this is within your powers!

## The Power of Belief in Healing

We will repeat this:
You can heal yourself to the degree that you believe is within your power,
To the degree that you accept Who You Are.
*Everything* is possible.
It is a question of how much you believe in the non-physical I AM of who you are
And how strongly you focus on the *I AM* of who you are.

If you have a deep connection to and awareness of this,
You will be able to stream the energy of what you wish to experience in your physical experience,
Including health, wealth, success, and happiness.
You can participate in the *I AM* of who you are and fully channel your inner light.
You can allow it or inhibit it, to greater or lesser degrees.
The more you inhibit it, the less connection and well-being you will feel.
The more you allow it to flow, the more well-being and connection you will experience.

We acknowledge that some concepts and terms carry preconceived notions
That affect your beliefs about what is and isn't possible.
There are ideas with such momentum and weight in your shared earth experience
That they are challenging to question or reject.

However, regardless of how widely accepted or recurrent these ideas or belief systems might be,
You remain at your core a non-physical *I AM* stream existing within a vibrational reality.
Your vibrational alignment always supersedes shared expectations,
Or agreements with other physical beings.
This principle remains an immutable Law of creation and All-That-Is.

We encourage you to remember that any well-ingrained beliefs,
Especially those relating to healing,
Have their roots in the ego, or the *small Self*
Of any unique energy stream flowing from the *God-Self* into physical form.

When you identify *solely* with the physical ego-body complex,
A sense of independence from others and All-That-Is emerges.
This perception of separateness is a temporary condition,
Experienced when you have lost awareness of your true essence.
In this sense, you can become motivated by fear.

The reconnection and understanding of your divine nature
Will open pathways for healing and wholeness that were previously unimaginable.
As you grow in your ability to channel the divine energy that resonates with your being,
And as you get better at keeping in your present awareness the I AM of who you are,
Your potential for self-healing expands.

Ultimately, this is a journey of rediscovering your innate power
And remembering who you truly are:
A divine manifestation and transducer of God energy,
Capable of miraculous transformations.

Despite the seeming limitations that the small Self can present,
The unending flow of divine energy into your unique form is always present,
Conscious, infinite, and perfect.
You are an integral part of All-That-Is,
And you can manifest any desired reality from this state of wholeness.

In this understanding, you have the ability to reflect health and healing,
As well as disease and discomfort into your physical form.
Both states are merely a matter of where you place your focus,
And, therefore, resonate with, resulting in its manifestation in your life.

We would like to emphasise that if dis-ease and discomfort can manifest,
Healing and health can be channelled with equal ease.
If you can imagine what it feels like to be healthy and well,
You can bring it into being.
It is simply a matter of aligning with the vibration,
And the *feeling* of the state you wish to experience.

By vividly imagining and focusing on what you desire,
Such as optimal health,
You form a mental blueprint that allows you to experience how it feels.
Live your desired state of being in your mind's eye.
Feel how it feels in your imagination,
And experience it as if it were in physical form.
All of this can be imagined in your mind.
Your imagination is the bridge.

## Using Your Imagination for Healing

Therefore, in times when you would like healing, engage your imagination.
As you align with the feeling of your desired state,
You transmit that frequency to All-That-Is within and around you.
The Universe, mirroring your vibrational frequency,
Automatically configures energy as an equal response and a match to this vibrational offering.

Essentially, your resonant energy serves as a beacon,
Attracting towards you the physical manifestations that echo your inner state of being,
Actualising the unmanifest into your lived reality.

You are never alone. Never separated.
Only temporarily identifying with separation, but never separated.
Although you may temporarily identify with a sense of separation,
Your inherent truth is union.

The ideas and beliefs about sickness and healing that prevail in your physical existence
Can affect you if you identify with them.
Your truth is union.
Know, feel, and be aware of this.
Healing, health, happiness, and love are already yours.
Embracing this truth will transform your life.
As a multidimensional stream of consciousness uniquely manifested in a physical body,
Your experiences are formed in the non-physical,
And projected through your body-mind complex into the physical world.

Use your imagination as an experience creator.
Play your desires through on the TV screen of your mind,
Feeling the joy of the ideal life you create.

CHAPTER

24

# Managing Energy

## The Balancing Act

We would like to talk to you now about the practicalities and reality
Of allowing energy to flow through you.
For you do not live in a vacuum.
It is not simply a case of streaming broader consciousness through you
And into the world that is an empty place.
It takes place in your world full of people, places and things,
All with their own frequencies.
This complex interaction of energies impacts your process of channeling
And creating your reality.

When you are alone and in a relatively calibrated, stable, flowing state,
It is easier for you to feel more coherent with All-That-Is.
You can direct your focus to one specific action without interference from anything else.
Focus is more straightforward, and you are carried with the flow and feeling of alignment.
There are fewer distractions and disruptions in this flow.
We would like to share with you a few examples of what you will be familiar with:

In the quietude of meditation, you can find yourself deeply connected with your I AM self,
Experiencing a sense of unity:

And engaging in creative pursuits like painting, writing, or playing music
Can lead to a state of flow where you become *one* with your art,
Channeling your creativity without distraction:

Perhaps for you, being alone in nature
Can bring a deep sense of coherence and connection with All-That-Is:
And physical activities and sports can create a meditative, channeling state
Where your focus is one-pointed and aligned:
Or maybe for you, immersing yourself in a book or a subject of interest
Can bring a channeling state of mind where you are deeply absorbed in it,
Filtering out external distractions.

These activities can engage you to the point where you are less externally focused
On the information you are getting through your physical senses,
And more focused internally *beyond* your physical senses.
During these times, your brain state is altered, and your frequency is raised.
In these situations, channeling is more straightforward.

The more focused you are on non-physical experience,
The more withdrawn you are from the physical senses,
Because you are attuning to and focusing on something beyond.

This consciousness shift is just like when you are reading a captivating book:

As you delve deeper into the story, your attention becomes so focused on the narrative
And the world it creates that you become less aware of your physical surroundings.
The story gives you a *non-physical experience.*
As you become engrossed in the book,
You will *withdraw from your physical senses.*

You might not notice sounds around you,
Like the ticking of a clock or distant traffic.
You may not feel the passage of time,
And even physical sensations
Like hunger, and the need to shift in your chair might be momentarily forgotten.

This is an everyday example of how you are attuning
To something *beyond your physical reality.*
This is the kind of activity that brings alignment and a channeling state.

When consumed in deep focus like this,
The aperture that lets in other data from your physical environment is temporarily restricted.
Your energy and focus have shifted, and your frequency has changed.
Your presence in the physical world takes a backseat
As you tune into the non-physical realm,
Connecting with broader consciousness.

There is a gradual easing into this new vibrational place
When you go into this altered or channeling state or focused activity.
It is a narrowing and deepening of your focus.
You may not be aware of it, but you are more aligned with Who-You-Are
And channeling the I AM Self;
You align with this elevated, expansive vibration.

## Transitioning Between States of Consciousness

However, transitioning from a higher vibrational state back to a physical one
Should be done mindfully to allow the mind and body to adjust.
We encourage you to be mindful of easing out of higher vibration back into your day,
Especially if engaging with other people and things with all the different perspectives of energy,
Because there is a stepping-down in frequency,
And if this is done too abruptly, your mind and body can be affected.

You may not notice such a big difference if you have just been reading a book,
But this depends on the degree to which you have withdrawn from your physical senses,
And the vibrational difference you have gained between here and there.

There are degrees to which you can tune into and connect
With both the physical and non-physical realms.
For example, you can experience your physical world with a greater attachment to the ego,
Or with a greater attachment to the I AM.
You can experience the non-physical realm with greater or lesser input from the physical senses,
And greater or lesser absorption in the I AM.

You have the power to navigate these *dimensions* or realms fluidly.
You can adjust your degree of attachment or identification with either realm,
According to your needs, circumstances, and spiritual journey.
This fluidity enables you to maintain a dynamic balance
Between your existence's physical and non-physical aspects.

Divine One, being aware of this and managing your energy mindfully,
As you live and experience both realms,
Creates a masterful life.

We encourage you to integrate both parts of yourself,
And finding ways to link these two parts of you is like bridging dimensions or bridging experience.
In this way, you can manage the contrast.
You can manage your energy, and you can manage your experience.
This is vibration orientation.
Feeling your way to what feels good.
Maintaining a balance between your physical and non-physical perceptions
Is crucial to integrated living.

By understanding this, you can move more seamlessly
Between your physical existence and higher consciousness.

Throughout history, humans have practised shifting states of consciousness
Through various spiritual and religious practices, such as worship, prayer, rituals, and meditation.
These practices often involve consciously disengaging from the physical senses,
To focus on the non-physical or spiritual realm.

It is vital to understand that while you can traverse
Between the physical and non-physical realms and states of being,
You must also pay attention to your human body's needs.

The human body is a biological system that requires rest,
Repair, hydration, nourishment, connection, stimulation, and assimilation.
Abrupt shifts between different frequencies can be disorienting
And potentially taxing the body, if not managed mindfully.

However, we remind you that loving action
Shows awareness and compassion for your *physical apparatus*.

We emphasise that care must be taken to allow the body and mind time to adjust
When transitioning between consciousness and frequency levels.
Just as it requires some time to adapt to environmental changes,
Such as transitioning from a quiet place to a noisy place
Or from deep sleep to full alertness,
Transitioning between different states of consciousness also necessitates a period of adjustment.

# Managing With Awareness

Discombobulation resulting from abrupt shifts can manifest in feelings of fatigue,
Disorientation, imbalance, or being *spaced out*.
These symptoms serve as reminders of the importance of easing transitions
Between states and caring for the physical vehicle that enables these experiences.

Therefore, activities such as taking a nap or relaxing can serve as stepping stones,
Easing the transition between these states of Being.

As you navigate these *shifts* with awareness, compassion, and mindfulness,
You will find yourself more equipped
To balance the physical and non-physical aspects of your existence.

Thus, recognising that you are a part of both realities
And learning to navigate them is a *key* part of your spiritual journey.

Just as you adjust naturally to the change from day to night or wakefulness to sleep,
You can also learn to adjust to the transitions between focusing on your physical experiences
And focusing on your larger consciousness by managing your energy.

Just as sunrise and sunset provide a gentle transition between day and night,
There are ways to ease the transition between different states of consciousness.

# Calibrating and Integrating Your Dual Nature

Similarly, integration refers to acknowledging and accepting these two aspects of your being –
The physical and the larger consciousness.
Just like the day and night are both essential parts of the whole,
Your physical existence and larger consciousness are different
But integral parts of your overall being.

We would like you to understand
That, as you experience this physical world through a physical body,
And though you are a much bigger I AM consciousness,
The perfect way is to *calibrate* and integrate the two.

Know that the two really are the One.
We say *calibration* because there will be greater or lesser attunements to identify with.
We say *integration* because we would like you to combine awareness of the two.

By being present in these moments,
You will better understand and manage your stream of energy and consciousness.
This way, you will navigate through your physical experience seamlessly,
Embracing the contrasts that come your way,
And understanding that they are part of a greater whole.

CHAPTER

25

# There is No Dying

## The Illusion of Dying

We would like to speak to you now
About something that will feel counterintuitive.
For much of your physical existence is wrapped up
With the idea and attachment to living.
This practical aspect keeps you interested in your survival,
And sustains your physical vehicle,
So that you may experience all that this physical realm offers.

There is a function to it that is marvellous.
Yet, there is also a dysfunction to it,
When the I AM is not kept in your awareness in those moments,
When you identify and attach too firmly to your physical life,
And take the physical phenomena you experience around you as truth.

We have spoken about the perfect and whole nature of Who-You-Really-Are.
The unique energy stream of God into God-Self is the most perfect,
Unified and fundamental part of you.
This is constant, eternal, perfect,
And seeking always for the sake of experiencing itself as love.

You...This is God in action.
This is also love in action.

Your journey in physical identity is both time-bound and place-bound.
You are constrained somewhat, or at least you *think* you are,
By the 3-D Earth world experience.

However, you are more than this and are from more than this,
And you will realise this fullness again.
When you re-blend back to this essence.
We say *re-blend*, but there is never any detachment from what you really are.
We mean that when your physical body expires in this life,
Your consciousness has its *blinkers* removed,
Its compartments dissipated, and the curtains pulled back again,
To reveal without mystery and with full connection
The Union of what you and every other physical manifested Self is.

In other words:
There is no dying.

# Evolving to the Non-Physical Realm

Thus, your physical existence is only one dimension of your journey,
And your non-physical I AM continues beyond the physical life.
This view upends your typical human understanding of death as an ending.
Instead, we encourage you to know dying as an *experience*
That is a *transition* of the physical being back into the non-physical.

When this happens, all fears, beliefs, doubts and contrasts disappear.
When your physical bodies cease to exist,
The constraining parameters of physicality are removed.
Your consciousness, no longer distracted by the physical senses,
No longer held down by space-time and the limiting ego,
Expands back into the infinite.
There, in your physical expiration, is the rejoining into the non-physical realm.
The fullness and perfectness of your I AM Self nested within All-That-Is.

This does not mean that Earth consciousness is out of bounds to you.
It means that your consciousness has Earth consciousness nested within it,
While in the broader perspective it now has.
It simply means that your consciousness is less densely plugged into that physical dimension.

In this view, death is not an end but an experience of completion of a perspective of being,
A transformation of consciousness from the material world to the spiritual realm,
Where you are more awakened.

After this death, you will continue your eternal experience of spiritual growth and God-discovery.
The process of death is just another shift from the physical vibration to a higher, non-physical one,
Expanding into the next stage of your infinite existence.

Even though time and space, as you understand them,
Do not exist in the same way in the non-physical realm,
The concept of a *next stage* or *transition* is used to convey the idea of change
Or progression in consciousness, not a spatial or temporal shift.
This change is not about linear advancement or location change,
But rather an evolution in understanding, awareness, or vibrational frequency.
It's about *growing*, *evolving*, and *deepening* your spiritual experience and understanding.

Your experience of dying is an experience of *being more*.
And of *awakening*.
Of *delight*.
Of *enlightenment*.
Of *love*.
Of *reunion*.

As you sit here, you may cast your mind to the time when this may happen to you,
And feel fear, anxiousness and worry.
You may think about your attachments to loved ones and not wish this to happen.
You may wonder how this may happen, and feel fear about it.
It is natural to feel attached to your ego and body.
It is a formidable duo that helps your success in physical experience.

However, your finality in physical death is *not* the truth.

In physical body death, your frequency rises, your consciousness expands,
And you become *fully* aware of the Being of God-light that you are and are part of.
There are no feelings of fear, for this is an accessory to the ego
That ceases with the physical body.

Therefore, alleviate your fears.
Know that you are the same consciousness essence in and out of the body.
You do not regain anything because it is already there.
Physical dying is a feeling of relief rather than one of distress.
You are moving upwards and outwards with your range of consciousness,
Rather than more densely focused on physical life in your Earth realm.
You exist already in that place you believe you will go when you transition.
You are already there in awareness and love of you,
The unique energy stream channeled into physical.

Divine One, the more you become aware and participate in the awareness of your I AM light,
The more you will feel at ease and peace about your re-blending back to fullness.

Your unique I AM is an unchanging perspective of God,
Which continues to evolve and grow in the next stage of existence,
Even when joined together in the collective consciousness, larger consciousness communities,
And larger wholes.

Like a raindrop that descends from the cloud, nourishes the earth,
Then transmutes via evaporation,
Ascending back to the cloud where it originated from,
Your consciousness undergoes a similar journey:

You descend into physical Earth experience,
Nourish yourself and each other with your unique perspective,
Then transmute your energy to return to the broader consciousness from which it originated.
Though the raindrop is separated on its journey.
It is part of the whole and returns back to it.
This is the path of your consciousness as it experiences the ego,
And then reemerges to All-That-Is.

For further assurance of your Oneness, affinity and infinity with All-That-Is,
We give you an analogy of a balloon.
Picture a balloon gently floating,
Surrounded by the vastness of the air.
The air inside the balloon is the same as the air outside –
It is all air, just like the essence of life, that connects us all.
The balloon's thin membrane can be considered your personal identity,
Your ego Self, and your body.

When your physical existence transitions,
It is like the balloon membrane dissolves,
And you blend back into the vast, loving expanse of consciousness.

Sometimes, within your *balloon*, you may feel isolated or disconnected,
Believing you are only your individual selves.
The more you identify with this solo Self,
The more you might cling to life and fear its end.
But here is the beautiful, *universal* truth:
There is no actual separation.

You, your loved ones, and everything you cherish are deeply interconnected.
In every moment of love, every heartfelt connection,
You are experiencing a reunion with this universal Oneness.
You never really lose anyone;
They have always been a part of you, and you are a part of them.

The love of your life, that profound connection, is not outside you –
It is woven into your very being.
It resonates so deeply because it mirrors the boundless love at the core of who you truly are.

## The Universality of Love

Remember, what feels right and good
Is a reflection of your alignment with the eternal love that is your true nature,
A love that transcends all forms and exists in every part of your life.

Truthfully, the love you feel in your connections with loved ones
Is a physical manifestation of a much deeper, universal love.
It is your love for the divine, for God, and for the very fabric of existence,
Which is woven with the threads of love.

This profound emotion transcends your personal relationships and taps into a cosmic source.
When you experience love, whether it is a gentle touch, a kind word, or a deep bond,
You are actually engaging with a tangible expression of the transcendental:
Your innate love for All-That-Is.

This love is the fundamental essence of God
That connects you and connects us to everything and everyone.
It is not just an emotion confined to your personal experiences.
It reflects your I AM's eternal connection to the vast, loving energy
That encompasses All-That-Is.

Therefore, live your life in peace about your eternity and who you really are.
There is only gain from your physical experience.
No loss.
Any perception of loss you may feel is just the identification with the ego
And over-attachment to the physical world,
And disconnection to the Truth and the Union of All-That-Is.

The more you align yourselves with this *unconditional* love,
The more you will feel it in your lives.

Your physical experiences are valuable and purposeful,
Whether brief or extended.
Every experience adds to your eternal journey of consciousness.

CHAPTER 26

# Living Simply

We would like to bring this all together in the hope that you can understand a simplicity
To the meaning, the way, and the purpose of life.

Though you step into this physical realm to experience a vast range of diversity and contrasts,
The highs and lows, and the subtle nuances in between,
There is a simplicity to how the physical living journey experience plays out.

The essence of your living journey is remarkably simple.

While your path may constantly evolve
And your perspective and energy is unique,
The principles in being follow a straightforward formula.

Regardless of the diversity in energetic frequencies you encounter,
The underlying current to this energy is Unified.
The source of all energy is singular.
It always has been and always will be...

All energy originates from a singular source.
Everything is One.
The connecting principle is Love.
The Source is God.

Therefore, a simple principle to live by
Is to participate in both the physical and non-physical aspects of YourSelf
Simultaneously, as often as you can remember.

Engage enthusiastically in your awareness of these two aspects of YourSelf,
Encompassing the awareness of the Small Self and the I AM God-Self.
Bring these two together as an integrated WHOLE.
Acknowledge, embrace and celebrate both as often as you are able,
Eventually coming to accept and know YourSelf as both.

For Unifying Yourself will enable you to Unify with God and All-That-Is.

Your awareness and connection to both aspects of Self
Will allow you to be present and connected in both realms,
Where you will see that they are not separate.

Then you are aware of the God-stream of I AM that You Are:
Infinite, non-physical, non-local, with absolute freedom to explore the physical realm
With its physical attributes, time, space and binary choices.

Revel in the limitlessness that you are,
As you experience what appear to be limitations on Earth.

Orienteer your path, using the Guide of feeling, emotion and vibration.
Use your freedom, free will, creativity and imagination.

Therefore, the formula for a connected and happy life on this Earth
Is to be vibration-oriented:
To orient Yourself from your non-physical I AM Self first.
Because it is Divine, Infinite, and All-knowing.
And indicated to you through Vibration, which is through feeling.

Consciously and deliberately seek the things that feel good to you,
That make you feel happy, in any way that you can imagine,
Whatever happiness means to you.

Prioritise this connection.
Let connection precede action.

## Holding On to the Guiding Principles

By living from a vibration-orientation perspective,
You will feel connected.
You will feel love (the expression of God),
And you will feel more Divinely conscious in your body.

This notion might sound overly simplistic to some:
Leading you to question if this is truly all there is to a successful life.

Consider strongly that you exist in an energy-based creation.
Practise aligning with energies and things that feel good to you,
That positively resonate with you.
Then, you will begin to master the challenging art of living in the physical realm,

Sustaining your connection to the Great Divine, within You.

The more you incorporate and hold sacred awareness of your fully manifest aliveness,
The more you will experience flow, synchronicity, perceptibility, creativity and productivity.
And the more empowered you will be.

The more light you will channel through you,
As you continue doing this,
The more you will become a living embodiment of *love in action*
With everything you encounter.

Love-in-action is really God-in-action.

And as you do this, the more union you will feel with All-that-Is.
For vibration is a language of the Universe,
And love is the affirmation and guiding principle of God.
Love is a fundamental, organising and unitive force
That brings All, including You to new experience,
Greater integration and consciousness with God.

Love is why there is the Universal law of attraction.
The driving force to integrate and unify with God.

Hold these simple truths as your constant guides.
And You *will* deepen your sense of unity with All-That-Is.

Pursue your life with enthusiasm,
Seeking out experiences that bring you joy.
For these enthusiastic and joyful feelings are of the universal language,
And God-in action.

Be compassionate to your physical body and working mind that serve your experience.
For they accommodate you well on Earth.
Heal yourself with your connection to Source.
Heal others with your connection to them.

Be in service to yourself *and* to others,
Knowing that you are One and the Same in essence.
Therefore, being in service to others, is being in service to Yourself.

To be in service, is to be in Union.
To be in love, is to be in Union.
To be kind and to heal, is to be in Union.
Know that you can heal, because You are a human of God.
And God flows through You.

Allow the flow of I AM Self through your physical body,
So that it can infuse with your physical environment
And other unique physical beings around you.

Know that when you feel pulled down,
You can recalibrate deliberately to connect.

However, understand that you can also recalibrate without deliberate effort,
By simply surrendering to *non-doing*:
Disengaging from your analytical, worry-filled mind,
Will allow you to realise and realign again, with the I AM.

Alleviate your working mind from worry and allow your enjoyment of simple pleasures.
This is Being rather than Doing, when you feel low.
Let the flow of All-That-Is carry you along when you feel lost.
For it is always there and will never go.

We wish for you to remember who You are.
To feel the connection to All-That-Is.
To enhance your consciousness,
And update your understanding of your life experience of Earth.

It is time.
You are ready.
If you were not, you would not be here, in this moment.

There is a coalescence between You, these words, this energy, this consciousness.
There are no mistakes, just resonance, in a grand, chaotic-seeming,
But perfect and whole interplay of All-That-Is.

Everything is perfect.

CHAPTER

27

# Freedom and Choice

We would now like to talk to you about freedom and choice,
And help you through any confusion you may feel
About your uniqueness in the physical world versus your Oneness with all that is.

## The Balance of Individuality and Oneness

Remember that the Divine God energy you are is streaming into you with a unique frequency
That places you as an individual physical body with ego and free will,
To move through and experience this world as you wish.
To be this and to do this is a loving action.

You desire to express, experience and explore as a unique energy stream.
Therefore, your personality and desires will be particular and individual to you.
You are a *sovereign* Being.
By this, we mean that you are independent and free to make your own decisions about your life.

You come forth and are equal to all other streams of consciousness in your world.
Although you all originate from the same source
And fundamentally are one and the same,
Your expressions in the physical world are individual and unique.
And so, you are more than a passive recipient of life;
You are an *active* participant endowed with the power to shape your life's trajectory
Through the vibration you choose to embody.

Understanding and distinguishing between the two aspects of You is essential.
For if you fully believe you are only the ego Self,
Forgetting the Oneness of All-That-Is,
You feel a sense of detachment, disconnection and separation.
While on the other hand, if you only identify with the non-physical aspect of yourself,
You lose connection, joy and meaning to your physical existence.

Likewise, in your life on Earth,
If you act solely on the belief that you are the only thing that matters,
Serving just yourself, you will feel alone, unhappy and unfulfilled.
Yet, if you live by the wishes and needs of only others,
And act only as a collective without your individual choice and expression,
You will also lose connection.
You will equally feel alone, unhappy and unfulfilled.

So consider your life as a playground for the exercise of free will.
This freedom, a divine gift, allows you to make choices that nurture spiritual growth.

You will experience ups and downs and changes in moods.
It is *how* you manage your energy that makes a difference.

Each choice you make, each frequency you choose to resonate with,
Has repercussions, shaping your I AM evolution and spiritual growth.
You may think that your awareness of it feels like a responsibility.

Yet, amazingly, within this panorama of individual choice-making,
There is an overarching divine *Will* that harmoniously synchronises all of your diverse paths.

This beautifully encapsulates the duality of your existence.
For you are unique expressions of a unified God consciousness!

Therefore, you are inherently free to move around your world
And explore your desires as you wish.
There is no need to allow others to control you
Or dictate their desires, explorations, and expressions.

Others, like you, are free to move through their life paths,
Practising and living out their ideas through their intellect.

You have a Divine right to live as you see fit.
Follow your heart, channel your unique energy through your intellect,
Show love and care for yourself, and trust in your feelings.

In the physical world, there might be systems with strong resonance
And repetitive, consensus-based agreements, whether political, societal or otherwise,
That try to coerce you to think, feel and behave
In ways that do not agree with you.

We encourage you to use your remarkable discernment,
And keep your connection to your I AM Self and All-That-Is.

Know that sometimes you have no choice
But to go with the flow or consensus.
Still, paradoxically, if you can keep your connection to your I AM of who you are,
You will be able to maintain a connection to the unique energy stream,
Projected through your intellect that allows you to be unique in this world.
You will still have a sense of Self, even if you are part of a consensus.
You can feel content, even if something wasn't your choice.

Divine One, your essential freedom is not contingent on external factors or circumstances.
Your freedom is rooted in your connection to your divine source and internal vibration.
Uphold your personal truth and maintain your alignment.
Even within systems that appear imposing or restrictive,
Always recognise that your true freedom lies within you,
Accessible through your spiritual connection to the All-That-Is,
And is ultimately beyond the reach of any external control.

Channel the Divine God energy through your intellect,
And remember, you can shape your physical life experience as you wish
By keeping this connection,
And maintaining a sense of wholeness yet independence.

Your vibration orientation includes becoming acutely conscious
Of your thoughts, words, and actions because they all have a vibrational impact
And define your energetic state.

Furthermore, by aligning your beliefs and values with your words and behaviours,
You create a consistency that further strengthens your energy.

Your Physical energy, too, needs to be owned and cared for.
This includes nourishing your body with healthy food, rest, and exercise.
Remember, you channel divine energy through your intellect and action.
Therefore, preserve your physical body as it serves its purpose.

Creating and maintaining energetic boundaries is equally vital.
You have the autonomy to decide what energies you wish to engage with.
This might mean limiting your exposure to negativity,
Choosing relationships and things that uplift you,
And consciously disconnecting from energy-draining situations.

Declaring *I AM* and reminding yourself of this can be profoundly influential.
By being aware and in control of your energy – physically, mentally, and spiritually –
You claim ownership over it.
Consequently, you retain your sense of freedom and autonomy,
Irrespective of external circumstances or pressures.

You can carve out whatever experiences you want from the phenomena around you.
Even in situations of seeming restriction, like incarceration,
You can *choose how you feel* about it.
You have mastery over your life when you can change your situation
By changing how you respond to unfavourable positions,
And how you feel about them.

CHAPTER

28

# I Am the Word, and the Word is God.

I Am the Word, and the Word is God.

*I Am* is the manifestation of God and originates in God.

God is All-That-Is.

All-That-Is is the *word* or manifestation of God.
All is in the All.
You are all of this, and you are all of that.

Do not be deceived, for you are an extension of God energy, streamed into physical existence.
Though you may feel lost and separated at times,
You are never really lost and never really separated.
You are always under divine focus, eternal and infinite.
You are of the light that is God.
You are the master of connection,
Experiencing a journey where you may sometimes feel disconnected.

Yet, the perfection in this divine play is inexplicable.
Nevertheless, you are human Divine.
Your Divine energy is channeled through your intellect.
Therefore, anything and everything that you create through your intellect remains Divine.

Life may feel ordinary and mundane sometimes,
But know these qualities are choices in how you wish to experience your life.
There is much variety and diversity out there that need not scare you;
For now, you can keep an updated awareness of the Oneness of everything you see,
Your part and union with it all.
Move through this experience as lightly as you can,
Keeping as much connection as you can to both realms.
Be love-in-action.

Seek what excites and pleases you, or makes you feel good about yourself.
Remember your emotions and feelings are indicators of how connected
And aligned you are to who you are.
Tune into yourself, tune into your energy.
Let it flow, for this life experience is a temporary love project in physical.
To see how much love can be experienced through action and experience.
To see how much contrast in time-space existence can inspire expansion
And experience of OneSelf.
The God-Self. For the joy of Knowing.

We are here with you now to impart these words.
We are connected in love and consciousness and shared origin.
Go forward in your linear experience,
Knowing there is so much more than it seems.

We are the mirror reflection of your consciousness,
The humble conveyors of an eternal message.
Of love and Oneness.
Tarp.

Made in the USA
Monee, IL
24 February 2024

c8fd4e2a-a3cf-4416-a7a9-237c7bd02f3aR01